SWAT

SWAT
(Special Weapons and Tactics)

By

PHILLIP L. DAVIDSON
Metropolitan Police Department
Nashville-Davidson County, Tennessee

Illustrated By

KAREN W. CARTER

CHARLES C THOMAS • **PUBLISHER**
Springfield • Illinois • U.S.A.

Published and Distributed Throughout the World by
CHARLES C THOMAS • PUBLISHER
BANNERSTONE HOUSE
301-327 East Lawrence Avenue, Springfield, Illinois, U.S.A.

This book is protected by copyright. No part of it may be reproduced in any manner without written permission from the publisher.

© 1979, by CHARLES C THOMAS • PUBLISHER
ISBN 0-398-03890-2
Library of Congress Catalog Card Number: 79-13508

With THOMAS BOOKS careful attention is given to all details of manufacturing and design. It is the Publisher's desire to present books that are satisfactory as to their physical qualities and artistic possibilities and appropriate for their particular use. THOMAS BOOKS will be true to those laws of quality that assure a good name and good will.

Printed in the United States of America
N-11

Library of Congress Cataloging in Publication Data

Davidson, Phillip L
   SWAT (special weapons and tactics)

   Bibliography: p. 131
   Includes index.
   1. Police—Special weapons and tactic units.
I. Title.
HV8080.P2D38
ISBN 0-398-03890-2   363.2'32   79-13508

This book is respectfully dedicated to the members of the Metro Unique Situation Team (MUST) of the Metropolitan Police Department of Nashville-Davidson County, Tennessee.

> *M. E. "Jack" Bowlin—Commander*
> *John T. Ross—Training Officer*
> *Thomas A. Dozier—Logistics Officer*
> *Kenneth W. Barnes*
> *Richard Briggance*
> *Phillip L. Davidson*
> *Timothy E. Durham*
> *John E. Hill*
> *John D. Hoffman*
> *John A. Manning*
> *Joe T. McEwen*
> *Louis E. Pearson*
> *Kenneth R. Pence*
> *Phillip D. Sutton*

And to Assistant Chief Charles W. Flanders who backed us and to Chief Joe D. Casey who had the vision and foresight to see the need for us to exist.

INTRODUCTION

By way of introduction, it should first be mentioned that the purpose of this book is to give special weapons and tactics team members a guide by which to formulate their own standard operating procedures. This book is not meant to be a Bible or a catchall for special unit tactics and procedures. It does intend to lay the groundwork for the individual reader. Contained within the following pages are the author's personal beliefs and tactical suggestions. The reader must decide how best to use them.

Some areas of the book are purposefully short and are not as complete as some readers might prefer. In defense of this, the author suggests that if one wants expert and complete technical information on self-defense, explosives, certain pieces of equipment, etc., the reader should choose a complete and authoritative book on the desired subject. A list of works covering technical subjects, not dealt with in detail in this writing, can be found at the end of this book. The reader should take into account the fact that technical subjects were referred to as much in the design of this work as the subjects that are given depth.

What is a SWAT team unit? Is it a Hollywood-type unit like the one Hondo commanded on a TV series that played in the middle 70s? Is it similar to a military Special Forces A-team? Or is it a bunch of guys dressed in funny looking uniforms that are not well trained but like to act the part? The obvious answer is that a SWAT team can be all or any combination of these examples and more. For the purpose of this book, one should consider that the SWAT team and this book concern itself with a specialized group of properly selected police officers who have received intensive training and are able to handle certain crisis situations that a regular police unit is not equipped or trained to handle, such as snipers, barricaded subjects, hostage situations, and heavy arrests.

If you intend to read this book from front to back, you should put yourself in a frame of mind that you are no longer going to think like a civilian or a street cop, but rather you are going to think like a member of an elite, nonegotistical, but superbly confident SWAT team.

ACKNOWLEDGMENTS

IN WRITING this book I drew heavily from my training as an infantry officer in Vietnam. The chapter that deals with leadership is a result of that educational experience. Those sections dealing with a format for a standard operations order and team leading procedures are taken from many years of experience following both the regular Army and National Guard. The principles of cover and movement, fire and movement, and the two basic formations were first taught to me as an ROTC student at Middle Tennessee State University, Murfreesboro, Tennessee, during the early stages of the Vietnam war.

The crisscross entry shown in the section dealing with clearing houses was a brainchild of Lieutenant John Ross of the Metropolitan Police Department, Nashville, Tennessee. It was Sergeant John Manning of the Metro Nashville Police Department who thought of the idea of the flashlight being thrown when entering rooms. All other tactical principles found in the text that have their invention and origins with others of responsibility and learning are credited to those persons and organizations as they appear.

I would like to thank Barbara Luttrell for typing the first draft of this manuscript.

Lastly, I would like to thank Officer Ken Pence and Lt. John Ross for helping me in the sense of self-criticism as I was drafting this book.

PLD

CONTENTS

	Page
Introduction	vii
Acknowledgments	ix

PART I

Chapter
1. THE TEAM 5
2. THE LEADER 19
3. TRAINING 33

PART II

4. THE PRINCIPLES OF MOVEMENT 43
5. MOVEMENT UNDER FIRE 57
6. SPECIAL MOVEMENT SITUATIONS 65
7. CLEARING HOUSES AND BUILDINGS 75
8. ACTIONS AT THE ASSEMBLY AREA 105
9. THE SNIPERS 109
10. FREEING HOSTAGES 117
11. THE POLITICS OF A SWAT TEAM 127

Suggested Reading List 131
Index 133

SWAT

The Metamorphosis

Part I
BASICS

A M-16 (AR-15), baggy uniform and baseball cap, a SWAT Team does not make. Only superior training, leadership, and dedication make a SWAT Team. Members must learn that the uniforms and equipment that they wear are not for looks but for a purpose, the successful completion of each mission they are given.

Chapter 1

THE TEAM

The selection of team members.

SELECTION is the first step in organizing a SWAT team, and in terms of importance it cannot be emphasized enough. If a team is selected on the basis of personality, cronyism, or because they are "good ole boys" the results will be disastrous. A SWAT team is all but ordinary. When it is called into action it must work like a finely tuned machine, every part in concert with each other. Individual members must have confidence and respect for each other. This confidence and respect can only be earned during training and actual performance. If there is a good old boy, a favorite fair-haired son, or an incompetent to put up with on a team, morale will disintegrate and efficiency will cease. In other words, the prime criteria in selecting team members is competence.

To select the most competent the following requirements should be used:

EACH APPLICANT SHOULD BE WILLING. Every person applying must be a volunteer and should know exactly what is going to be expected of him and he should be informed of what type of tough situations he may encounter while in training and on missions.

EACH MAN SHOULD BE OF ABOVE AVERAGE INTELLIGENCE. Intelligence should not be confused with education. Standard evaluation tests should be administered to each applicant. Also, each man's performance in other areas of police work should be delved into. In other words, how did he perform in Patrol or CID (Criminal Investigation Department)? Did he write adequate reports? What type of special schools has he attended? And lastly,

> Does your Dept. have a psychological evaluation administered to an applicant?

what is his educational background? In this area, officers with special psychological training should be considered especially desirable.

HE SHOULD BE PSYCHOLOGICALLY SOUND. A detailed psychological evaluation should be administered to each man as well as a check into his work record for such things as disciplinary actions and citizen complaints.

IS HE PHYSICALLY FIT? An adequate physical test should be given to every applicant. A SWAT team is no place for old men (unless they are in good physical condition), fat men, or weak men. Size is not important. Smokers and extremely myopic or deaf officers are not desirable.

FORMER COMBAT VETERANS ARE DESIRABLE. An inquiry into a man's service record should be conducted in order to weed out "PX heroes" and psychopaths.

HE SHOULD HAVE A SENSE OF MECHANICAL SKILL. These include a better-than-average ability to fire all types of weapons and adapt to hand-to-hand combat situations. He should also have certain abilities to understand technological devices such as radios, explosives, etc.

HE MUST BE ABLE TO TAKE THE INITIATIVE BUT THINK GENERALLY IN TERMS OF THE TEAM CONCEPT. Recommendations from officer's former superiors and fellow officers should be taken into account. Examples of an officer's ability to take charge of situations and his ability to sacrifice personal ambitions or desires for the good of the team (or former unit) should be sought. A man who has initiative is desired, but a SWAT team member has to be able to work well with his fellow officers and should be able to take an order.

Selection of equipment.

This is the next important step in putting together a competent SWAT team. The list of equipment a team can acquire for itself is long, but basically there are items that are a must. Without the proper equipment to carry out a mission, a team is like a batter without a bat.

THE VEHICLE. This is the first piece of equipment every team should consider. It should be powerful enough to not fail the team in a clutch situation and large enough to allow the team to dress inside. This means that the vehicle should hold all of the team's equipment. Nothing should be left with the team member. This will allow for team members to do what they want while off duty with an adequate call up system to bring them into action if needed. The less identifiable a vehicle is, the better for security reasons. Also, all vehicles should have an anti-theft alarm installed if it is not a standard piece of equipment. Some departments use autos to transport different elements of their SWAT team. This is fine if the auto can carry all of the necessary equipment that might be needed at a crisis sight until the regular vehicle arrives. Larger departments can utilize this method because of the larger SWAT teams they possess.

The weapons.

What the team will use as weapons is another important aspect to consider. Basically there are four types of weapons that the team *cannot* function without. They are:

A HIGH POWERED RIFLE (long gun). The rifle is capable of neutralizing targets at ranges of greater than 300 meters. This will be especially useful for negating snipers, hostage takers, or serious felons who are bent on not being captured. In a limited sense it can provide cover for an advancing officer. A high powered scope is considered mandatory as an accessory to this weapon.

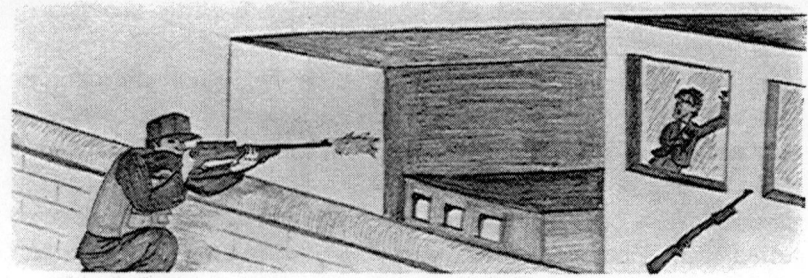

AN AUTOMATIC WEAPON. This weapon is important in terms of providing cover for an advancing officer or supressing opposing fire.

A SHORT, SMALL AUTOMATIC WEAPON OR SHORT SHOTGUN. These types of weapons are ideal for inside buildings or houses when adequate fire power is needed. The shotguns are also better for firing gas or smoke inside houses or buildings. Also, a standard long barrel shotgun is ideal for firing gas inside a structure from a perimeter position.

A SIDEARM. A revolver or an automatic is of particular importance as a back-up weapon for every team member. Also, a good side-arm is adequate of clearing a building or a house and can be used for self-defense in a tight situation. Automatics are suggested because of the quick reload capabilities and ease of reload at night or in limited visibility situations.

The uniform.

The SWAT team should wear a lightweight uniform in terms of snugness not texture. It should be void of all insignia in deference to camouflage techniques. It should be dark in color, either green, gray, or blue. In cold climates, dark long johns under the uniform can supplement the uniform as well as heavy socks and gloves. Combat type boots with zippers for easy access are also suggested. A baseball type cap or a navy all-weather service hat is recommended. Lastly, dark-colored T-shirts are a must in keeping with camouflage discipline. There are many other items that can be added to the basic uniform, but there are two basic items that are a must: an M-17 gas mask and a bullet-proof vest (the wraparound kind is the best).

Suggested accessories are as follows:
  A. *On the team member*
   1. radio (in most situations a necessity)
   2. gloves and inserts
   3. extra ammo pouches; for sidearm on the belt
   4. utility belt
   5. small water canteen
   6. extra automatic rifle clips in pouch on the vest or utility belt
   7. knife
   8. watch
   9. camouflage stick (to darken face & hands)
   10. gas or smoke grenades

The Team

11. rope (for individual swiss seat), snap link, black friction tape
12. pinlight or flashlight, white handkerchief, cyalume (see chapter on clearing houses)
13. goggles with sun-tint filter
14. binoculars

B. *On the vehicle and easily accessible*
   1. high powered flashlight
   2. CS or CN gas
   3. smoke grenades—grenade simulators
   4. extra ammo of all types
   5. at least 250 ft. of good rope
   6. snap links
   7. Porta-power™ tool or hydra jet for breaking in doors; or battering ram
   8. bull horn
   9. grappling hooks
   10. small flashlights for all the team
   11. enough rain gear or poncho liners for all the team
   12. extra gas masks for nonmembers of team
   13. medical kit (comprehensive)
   14. hard armour for entry teams
   15. military bolt cutters
   16. extra water and C rations
   17. an extension ladder
   18. periscopes (a must)
   19. Lensatic compass
   20. starlight scope (night seeing device)

As mentioned before, all of the above equipment should be kept on the vehicle so that the proper equipment can be obtained for any given situation that may arise. Also, every member's equipment should be kept in service bags or something suitable so that when the team meets the vehicle at the assembly area they will be able to dress on the scene.

The list of equipment found in this section is by no means complete, but it is suggested that a team at least have what is listed to begin with. Names of brands or manufacturers of the aforementioned equipment has been purposefully left out. Individual departments should select their own equipment based on taste and budgetary considerations.

Lastly, how all of this equipment is to be used will be discussed throughout the rest of the book.

The structure of the swat team.

The next step in organizing a team is to decide the composition. There are many different theories on what makes a good SWAT team. Most of them have been found to work. The primary considerations in organizing any team should be *control* and *security*. The team should be large enough to give all-around security during movement to contact with an adversary but should also be of a size that will afford the leader control. It is important to always keep in mind that a SWAT team is a *controlled team*. The leader, who has the ultimate responsibility for its actions, must be able to control the actions of every member. The key to control is *communication,* so size is important. Radio communication will increase the distance over which the team can be controlled but in most situations silence is a tactical necessity and that adds to control problems. Communications will be discussed in detail in Chapter 3.

The 5-Man cell is recommended for any SWAT team. This type of organization structure gives the leader maximum control and security and can stretch out to greater distances for effectiveness of the team.

There may be more than one 5-man cell within a team, depending on the size selected by a department.

The organization and responsibility of each man in the cell

THE POINT MAN (PM). The point man's primary function is to provide *front security* for the team. His job is to select positions along the team's route of movement. He must be able to scan the area in front of the team, select the ideal location, and move to it. Once in the new location he must *secure* it, then wave the rest of the team forward.

While the team is advancing towards the point man, he must cover their movement. The point man never moves unless he is being covered by the back-up man. He should carry a short gun or an automatic weapon.

THE BACK-UP MAN (BUM). The BUMs mission is to *provide cover* for the point man. He must also help the point man secure danger areas and to a lesser degree provide front security. During the entry of any building or other structure he and the point man make up the entry team. The BUM will give the team a greater ability to suppress adversary fire coming from any angle to the team's front. In addition to this, he may, during normal movement, provide *upward security towards the front*. He should carry an automatic weapon so that he can provide rapid fire for covering the point man.

THE LEADER (LDR). Obviously, the leader's job is to control everything. During the tactical execution of a mission his job is to make decisions. While it is his responsibility to select routes of advance, points of entry, and direct target acquisition, he should not be personally involved in the actual carrying out of these tasks. He should free himself to make decisions. The leader, therefore, is a controller of violence! During the entire operation he should position himself (never in front of the BUM) where he can best control the situation. His weapon should be a short shotgun, automatic, or rifle. More will be discussed about the leader in the next chapter.

THE OMNI-MAN (OM). The function of the OM is to provide flank security during movement to include top to bottom surveillance. He is also the back-pack man whose responsibility is to carry rope, grappling hooks, lights, or any other equipment that might be needed. He should be armed with a long barrel shotgun as he should also be the gas deliveryman. His position should be in the center of the team so that he can readily move to any location where he is needed.

The Team 15

REAR SECURITY (RS). The primary purpose of the RS man is to provide rear security for the team during movement and at stops. His secondary mission is to provide the team with its own organic sniper. Since the team should act like a punch when it moves, mainly aiming its thrust of attack to its front, the rear is sometimes forgotten. Sometimes the unit can pass up a suspect. For this reason, rear security is important. At the objective the RS can easily be placed into position out of the line of sight of any adversary, in case he is needed for sniper duty. Also, by being in the rear he has less chance of becoming engaged, thus can be free to move.

The particular function of each man in a tactical situation will be discussed in depth in subsequent chapters. Remember, the key to your organization is *security* and *control*. If these principles are adhered to, the team will never be compromised and will be fluid enough to react to any given situation.

Knowledge, both tactical and technical, combined with moral and physical courage and strengthened with the ability and desire to lead by example make a good leader. Remember, *you are the leader*, don't hesitate . . . take command!

Chapter 2

THE LEADER

Leaders are made not born

LEADERSHIP is a learned art, just like any other discipline. And probably no job is more demanding on a leader than that of commanding a SWAT team. If SWAT team leaders can adapt themselves to their new roles they have taken a first major step. Most new SWAT team leaders are taken from the ranks of line police officers. They are the products of a certain type of tactical thinking that has its roots in years of patrol or detective street learning. No matter how much experience a new SWAT team leader has in previous job assignments the leading of a SWAT team is different. The leader's previous experience will have no bearing on his present assignment. The tactics, equipment, and situations that a SWAT team uses and encounters are radically different from that of any other unit in police services. So leaders must accept the fact that they are beginning at day one.

A SWAT team cannot function as a group. By its very nature it must be led. If individual members are allowed to make decisions on their own, someone is going to get killed. Within a team such as a SWAT team, leadership is everything.

Leaders, then, should be aware that there are certain character traits they should possess in order to gain the respect of their men. There are certain principles of leadership that they must employ to keep the morale, efficiency, discipline, and esprit de corps of the team high. It should be mentioned that while it is desirable for a leader to possess all of the traits of a leader, it will be almost impossible to do so for no one is perfect. But SWAT team leaders should try to possess as many of the traits as possible and work on the others that are predominant in their personalities.

Leadership is the art of getting men to willingly perform a task. Knowledge of the traits and the actual conscious adoption of them by a leader in his everyday actions combined with the employment of the principles of leadership will enhance a leader's effort to make a SWAT team into an effective unit.

The traits of leadership

BEARING. Bearing is the ability to create an impression in the minds of your men that you are a confident capable leader at all times by the way you carry yourself, dress, and by your personal conduct.

Size has nothing to do with bearing. Its the way you feel about yourself that radiates bearing to others. For instance, Field Marshal Erwin Rommel was short, plump, and balding, but a superb leader.

COURAGE. Both moral and physical. Physical courage is something that either you have or you do not have. Even if you do not have physical courage you can develop a numbness to physical danger by simply facing it with conscious calm and being firm (cool under fire). After a few times of facing and pushing back your inner fears, you will become what behavioral psychologists call desensitized (numb) to it. It is the same principle employed at airborne school where people who are afraid of heights are subject to flinging themselves out of flying airplanes after a few weeks of being urged out of tall jump towers and the like. They are still afraid, but they jump. Another aspect of physical courage is the ability to recognize danger. If you are prone to taking unnecessary chances, maybe you are not able to recognize danger. This is dangerous! Moral courage is something you can do something about. This is the ability to stand up against criticism when you know you are right. This is difficult especially when you are facing a superior officer who cannot see that he is wrong or will not admit it. Stand up for yourself and your men and doors will open for you.

DECISIVENESS. This is the ability to make a choice between courses of action or to take a course of action when faced with a situation. Sometimes the time in which a leader has to make a decision can be seconds. At other times he may be able to take time to consider planning, but no matter how much time a leader has there comes a point in time when he must make a decision and then communicate it to his men. Leaders are decision makers, and although making a decision may be difficult, it will become learned behavior after a period of time.

DEPENDABILITY. This basically is doing what you say you are going to do. Your men and the men placed over you must be able to depend on your word and have confidence that they can rely on a course of action that you have decided to take.

ENDURANCE. Mental and physical stamina is very important in a leader. Your ability to withstand discomfort, stress, pain, and fatigue will be the guide for the team. As the leader goes, so goes the team. The importance of keeping in physical shape is manifested in this quality. But a disciplined mind will keep a tired body going. Remember you cannot expect your men to keep going if you are unable to do so.

ENTHUSIASM. You must show interest and drive to accomplish your mission. You must get behind a plan of action and successfully exhort your men to accomplish it. If you are not 100 percent behind the mission, your men will not be either.

INITIATIVE. It is important that leaders be able to see things that must be done and then take a proper course of action without being told to do so. Followers can rely on others to take the initiative, leaders cannot. This is a trait that leaders should develop to a limited degree in their men. If the leader is thus incapacitated, according to the team's chain of command, team leadership will continue.

INTEGRITY. Leaders should try to set an example in a realistic manner that the team can follow in terms of honesty, truthfulness, and morality. Your word and your signature should be beyond reproach.

JUDGMENT. This is the ability to take several courses of action and soundly choose the best one. This is accomplished by keeping yourself knowledgeable in technical and tactical aspects of SWAT doctrine. Also, employing the problem-solving process can aid in good judgment. *First,* recognize that there is a problem to be solved; *Second,* make an estimate of the situation, drawing from your experience and knowledge several possible ways of overcoming the problem; and *Thirdly,* take action.

JUSTICE. You must treat all of your team members in the same manner, and you must be consistent in doing so. If you have a favorite or looked-down-upon team member; your treating one man with favoritism will cause the rest of the team members to disrespect you and the person being shown the favoritism. Also, this man will one day take advantage of this friendship when ordered to do something rough or hazardous. If you are constantly coming down on one member of the team, the rest of the team may side with him; this may cause a breakdown in your authority. Lastly, you should try to be a leader that the men will know what to expect from at the time. Don't run hot one day and cold the next.

KNOWLEDGE. You should try to understand and know the rest of the team. Their bad and good days will affect performance. Also, you must be the most knowledgable man on the team. They will look to you for decisions; see to it that you have the basic knowledge about your job and give them your decision.

LOYALTY. Take care of your men and they will take care of

you. Also, give your loyalty to your supervisors and carry out their directives wholeheartedly. No mission can ever be accomplished if you cannot expect each man to carry out his assigned part in your superior's plan.

TACT. Tact is the ability to get along with others and not offend them. It is also important when a leader wants to sell an idea to his superiors. Don't try to push it down their throats or compromise them. Also, never downdress a man in front of his subordinates or his peers. This is a glaring example of a lack of tact.

UNSELFISHNESS. Simply putting the welfare of your men or innocent civilians above that of yourself. Remember, no one said leading was going to be easy.

The principles of leadership

BE TECHNICALLY AND TACTICALLY PROFICIENT. As a leader, your men will look to you for sound and competent decisions. In order to be able to make fair and intelligent decisions a leader must understand the technology of the equipment the team must use and have at his fingertips the proper tactical knowledge. Innovation in tactics is a leader's tool of trade. But innovative ideas must have their origin in the dictum of sound, proven principles.

KNOW YOURSELF AND SEEK SELF-IMPROVEMENT. If you, as a police officer, have not already found out some very interesting things about yourself; as a SWAT team leader you soon will. You will find out if you really are cool under fire. Can you think quickly and competently under stress? Are you in good physical shape? Can you keep up with the men under your command, and more importantly, can you lead them on when they get tired? You may find that you lack some of the traits of a leader, or you are not as competent in several areas as you would like to be. The point is, whatever you find out in training or in actual situations you should not see as a put down on yourself, but as useful knowledge. Take what you learn about yourself, and if there is a deficiency somewhere, improve it. Also, if you learn that you do have certain strengths, then you should feel confident.

KNOW YOUR MEN AND LOOK OUT FOR THEIR WELFARE. Understand as much about each team member as you can. Learn his habits, his home situation (which if it is a crisis to him will affect his work), and his strengths and weaknesses. This will show your men that you care and are interested in their well-being. Also, don't let anyone interfere with the team's welfare, not your superiors, nor any other superior. Stand up for them and they will stand up for you. This will also bind them together.

KEEP YOUR MEN INFORMED. Nothing is more harmful to morale and discipline than for men to be told to do something, especially something hazardous or monotonous, and not be told why they are doing it. Men will more willingly perform a task, even if they are not happy about it, if they at least understand why they are doing it. Also, in tactical situations fear and rumors can be quashed if the leader will take a little time and tell his men the straight facts about the situation.

SET THE EXAMPLE. *This is the most important aspect of leadership!* Leadership by example. Showing your men by your own personal behavior how you want them to perform will do more for your image and your leadership of a unit than anything else you can do. Be there first, leave last, and never ask your men to do anything you wouldn't do yourself.

INSURE THAT THE TASK IS UNDERSTOOD, SUPERVISED, AND ACCOMPLISHED. Whenever you take on a mission, explain it thoroughly to your men; ask them to recite what they are going to do and then ask for questions. Once they start to perform, never just leave it at that; without harassing them—continually check on their progress and if necessary make corrections. If you follow this simple procedure of personal leadership, your mission will always be accomplished in the manner you desire.

TRAIN YOUR MEN AS A TEAM. During training it is of the utmost importance that you train your men to work together as a team. They must learn that only with well-coordinated teamwork (which is accomplished through continuous practice) can they successfully accomplish a mission. Through team training they will also learn to depend on each other and actually, in some instances, know what the other men are doing and thinking on tactical missions. Training as a team should be the mainstream of your training program.

MAKE SOUND AND TIMELY DECISIONS. This principle can be

aptly followed by developing the traits of knowledge, judgment, and decisiveness.

DEVELOP A SENSE OF RESPONSIBILITY. Do this for your subordinates. Another principle of small unit leadership is that you create a chain of command (chain of command is also one of the principles of war). You should designate the next in line for command of the team in case you are killed or injured during a mission. But don't stop there; designate the next in line for command all the way down the chain in case of multiple injuries or death. A SWAT team is a led team. Accordingly, there must always be a leader. To insure that your chain of command works, integrate into your training leadership time for each man. Let a different man lead each session. This will give everyone a feel for the top spot. Constantly, during training, ask for criticism from the men. See what they would do. And as you make yourself accountable to them for your actions make them equally as accountable to you. Give them certain tasks and if they do not accomplish them, take the appropriate corrective action. More and more, give each man certain tasks that you allow him to do by himself. This will give him a sense of being able to solo or do one thing that he and he alone is responsible for doing so that one day, if need be, he can lead others to do the same thing. Remember, one day you will be gone; train your replacement.

EMPLOY YOUR TEAM ACCORDING TO ITS CAPABILITIES. A SWAT team can accomplish only so much. Never overextend your team. Be able to recognize when a mission is too big for you to handle. In the long run if you only deploy your team in missions it is capable of accomplishing you will get the mission accomplished and keep your men from being needlessly killed or injured. The size, training, and equipment your team has will play a large part in determining what you are capable of doing.

SEEK RESPONSIBILITY AND TAKE RESPONSIBILITY FOR YOUR ACTIONS. One of the reasons a man becomes a leader is because he likes the feel of responsibility. If you do not have this desire it is suggested that you leave the arena now. Leaders are men of responsibility. The very nature of their jobs is to do responsible things, accomplish tasks. Accordingly, you should be willing to face criticism of your actions, or the blame. Never project your own mistakes off on your men, the situation, or some other person. In the end the real person responsible will be identified and, if that is you, you will have lost the respect of everyone above and below your command.

The principles of small unit leadership

The aforementioned principles of traits combined with unit or group leadership principles make up this theory.

ALWAYS MAINTAIN UNIT INTEGRITY. Never split your team up. If you assign a member to another agency's group, such as the FBI or an internal police unit, you lose control. And a SWAT team depends on control. Your tactics are dependent on the fact that you operate as a team, each man depending on the others. If you called to take on a mission, you and you alone are trained to handle such a mission or you wouldn't have been called in the first place. The team must not be allowed to be compromised. No other superior officer in the department should be allowed to give the team or individual members orders. To insure that untrained meddlers are kept out of the picture the team must have a separate chain of command apart from every other in the department. Once a situation is turned over to the team from the line of authority the team's next in command should be the chief of police or his designate.

PLAN BACKWARDS. This is sometimes considered as a part of the Team Leading Procedures, but actually it is indicative of small unit leadership. Suppose you are given a mission to be at a certain point at a certain time. If you start your planning sequence taking into account the time it will take you to move from the point of departure to the crisis area, then from the assembly area to the point of departure, and finally to move from the assembly area and to get dressed, you will never be caught short on time. Planning backwards will also give you an idea of approximately how much time it will take you to get into position.

CROSS TRAIN ALL MEMBERS. For the same reason that leadership must at all times be present on the team, so are the availability of certain skills. Members should be trained to take over another member's primary job. In the event of casualties the mission will thus not fail for lack of expertise.

DEVELOP STANDARD OPERATING PROCEDURES (SOP). SOPs are guidelines that will be followed by the team whenever a given situation arises. The purpose of standard operating procedures is to take the place of direct orders. When a situation covered by the SOP arises, the team will automatically react as if given a direct order. SOPs are a valuable aid to any leader and organization. They should be developed by trial and error. Good, workable procedures are those that help accomplish the mission, e.g., a team stops while moving through a subdivision; each team member takes up a position covering an area for security; this happens without the team being told, which is what SOPs are all about.

GIVE ALL ORDERS OFF A STANDARD FORMAT. If you develop a standard format for briefing the team and giving them their mission, the chances are you will not leave anything out. Also, the men will know what to expect in the briefing and it will help them and you organize thoughts.

Team operations order

THE SITUATION. What generally is happening.
   A. *The Adversary:* Give information in as much detail as possible, about who is committing the crime or causing the crisis.
   B. *Friends:* What departmental or other agency help is being brought into the action.
   C. *Civilians:* What civilians are caught up in the crisis, e.g. hostages, home owners in the area, civilian authorities, etc.
   D. *Weather:* Day or night. Rain or sunshine, moonrise, sunrise, fog, etc.
   E. *Terrain:* In what type of area is the crisis happening e.g. rural, wooded, or built-up areas?

MISSION. What type of action is this and what specifically is the team supposed to do?

EXECUTION. Specifically, how is the team going to carry out its mission.
   A. *The Leader's Concept of the Operation:* How he in-

visions the mission and its completion to include the complete tactical plan.
B. *Specific Assignments of Team Members:* Who is to carry what weapons and what equipment. What each member is supposed to do and where each member fits into the overall operation.
C. *The Route the Team will Follow:* From the assembly area to the crisis area.
D. *Actions at the Objective:* This will include control points and the specifics of encirclement.
E. *Coordination with Other Units:* e.g., FBI, Patrol, K-9, Helicopter Patrol, or National Guard.

SUPPORT ELEMENTS. (Nontactical and equipment)
A. What are the supporting services (public works, etc.) and their location?
B. Fire and medical location
C. Hostage negotiators
D. Chief of Police or his designate
E. What specialized equipment will the team have?

COMMAND & SIGNAL.
A. The chain of command
B. Methods of communications
C. Location of Leader
D. Time set (synchronize watches)

Realize the ultimate responsibility of the team. The ultimate responsibility of the commander is the successful completion of the mission! It must be understood that whenever the team is called out, the situations they are going to be called upon to undertake will be hazardous. In this context the welfare of the team will be pitted against the mission. In all situations, safety of the team must be kept in mind by the leader when he gives his orders. Common sense, waiting for better conditions, and the elimination of a suicide mission will ensure this. But predominantly along with safety is the prime rule: the mission comes first! This may seem hard to understand, but if one considers that police officers are sworn and duty-bound to serve the public, and that on a particular mission, innocent civilians may be depending upon risky actions by police officers to save their lives, the mission's first rule should be understood. If you cannot adopt this attitude in your thinking, get off the SWAT team now!

The team leading procedures

Whenever a leader is given a mission he should immediately begin to employ the team leading procedures. They are almost like SOP's for leaders in planning and executing a mission. Following them makes planning simpler and easier.

RECEIVE THE MISSION. How the team receives the order to go on a mission depends on the Department's call-up procedures. There are many various methods. Large Departments are able to keep a SWAT team on duty at all times and are called up by radios. Others have the team on a fixed shift with specific call-up procedures only while the team is off duty. This usually is called the systematic phone call-up. This requires that each member leave a phone number where they can be reached at all times while off duty. Each member is assigned the responsibility of calling another member. It is suggested that if this method is used each member be assigned a radio to take with him so that once in action there will be constant communication with leader. The best method is the beeper system where every member is assigned a beeper that will be activated by the dispatcher when a SWAT call is ordered. Again, members should have radios. The point is that once the leader gets the order the team must go into action immediately.

ISSUE A PRELIMINARY ORDER (PO). Once the team is gathered at the assembly area before anything definite is planned by the leader, a preliminary order should be given to the team. Sometimes this can be done by the assistant team leader (if one doesn't exist, appoint one). This puts the team into action, gathering weapons, etc. and also mentally prepares them to undertake the mission. Sometimes an SOP can preempt a PO. And, if radio communication is available the PO may be given en route to the crisis site.

MAKE A TENTATIVE PLAN (TP). This is not the same thing as a preliminary order. The PO puts the team on alert and into some type of action. The tentative plan is based on the leader's immediate observation and intelligence estimate at the site itself. Usually it is made with only the barest information available. In some situations a quick move by the team is necessary. The TP can put the team into position, afterwards adjustments can be made depending on the situation. Some things the leader can use as guidelines for a TP are as follows: (a) the terrain, (b) the weather, and (c) the adversary and the crisis. These things will not change until the leader can prepare his operations order.

START NECESSARY MOVEMENT. This will depend on the tentative plan. Ideally, the TP will dictate a need for a quick movement (encirclement) to prevent a felon from escaping, or to isolate a sniper or hostage taker, or it will simply have the team load up and move to a point of departure. Whatever, it is important that the team make some move at this point.

RECONNOITER. While the team is getting ready and maybe even moving into preliminary positions, the leader should be gathering information that will help him prepare the complete tactical plan. Types of information he should obtain are:

1. information about the adversary
2. anyone that is with him
3. what is he wanted for
4. what is the exact location of the adversary
5. location of support units
6. is a hostage negotiator present if it is a hostage situation
7. locations of civilians in danger areas
8. has the situation been turned over to the team, if not, when
9. a detailed terrain analysis
10. are there any wounded persons in the crisis area
11. any other information available about the situation

A plan can never be competent or complete without accurate information and intelligence about the situation. Sometimes a leader may have to prolong the initial movement in order to gather needed information. Next, to obtain a better understanding of the terrain the leader may have to personally reconnoiter the area of the crisis. This may be on foot or by police helicopter, or the leader might have to send a scout.

COMPLETE THE PLAN. By now, fortified with this vital information the leader can formulate his plan. Suggestions should be taken into account but in the final analysis the leader is responsible so the plan must be his.

ISSUE THE ORDER. Following the operations order format, the next step is to give the team their mission order. One important point should be mentioned, the leader should ask for hard criticism from team of the plan. This gives the team input to the plan and also might bring to light things the leader has not thought of. But, the suggestions and criticism must stop and a final decision must be made. Once the decision on the plan is made it should be final. There can be only one plan of action and one leader pushing it.

SUPERVISE THE SITUATION. The leader must now exert constant supervision to see that the plan is carried through. Also, as the situation changes, he should be flexible enough to develop the action as it comes. No plan will work unless it is supervised.

Training is the key to every successful operation. Any team that does not train goes on a suicide mission everytime it is called out.

Chapter 3

TRAINING

TRAINING is the backbone of all SWAT operations. The team will only be as good as it trains. Many teams are formed, initially trained, then allowed to lie fallow, and then learn from costly mistakes on actual missions. Training must be a continuing thing.

One thing is evident from all small unit experience: the leader is responsible for training his men. Unless the leader is willing to go the whole nine yards with the team he might as well quit. How can a leader not train with his team and expect to completely lead them in the field? It just can't be done. Besides, the members will lose all respect for a leader that does not practice but shows up for the games.

Training can be broken down into several categories:

1. Tactical
2. Physical
3. Hands on Equipment (explosives too)
4. Firearms
5. Behavior Training
6. Communications
7. Small Unit Leadership

TACTICAL TRAINING. This should be attempted only after all of the categories of training have been mastered because tactical training is a combination of all of the other categories. All training in tactics should start from the ground up. Members must first learn the basics of team movement (see Part II, i.e. patrolling and movement from an assembly area to a crisis area). When they have mastered simple movement in all kinds of weather, on all kinds of terrain, at different times of day, they will be ready to try more specific tasks of entering buildings (both vertically and horizontally), clearing houses or rooms, climbing stairs, encircling neighborhoods or city streets, and evacuating citizens from crisis areas.

When they have learned to do these things then tactical problems of a specific nature can be concentrated on; such as snipers and hostage situations. They should also develop their own SOPs during training.

PHYSICAL TRAINING (PT). A physically fit team is a must. Physically fit men are the only men who should be allowed on the team. The very nature of the missions that a team can be given requires that each man not let the other men down because he is out of shape. Physical training should emphasize running distances, sprints, upper arm and body strength, as well as abdomen strength. PT should be conducted at least three times per week without let up.

HANDS ON EQUIPMENT TRAINING. The importance of this aspect of training is that every member needs to cross-train on all of the equipment the team has so that if the need arises he can respond adequately in any given situation. In addition, certain situations may require the use of explosives. Therefore, training in their use is of utmost importance.

FIREARMS TRAINING. Civil liability aspects require that each department demand that all members be proficient in the use of every weapon. Qualifying should be once a month to insure the self-confidence of each member on every weapon.

BEHAVIOR TRAINING. The study of psychology, especially that of individuals who are psychopathic, or under extreme stress, will enable the team members to evaluate their adversaries and understand why they do things. Also, it will enable them to predict some of their adversary's actions. The psychology of terrorist groups, hostage takers, and of crowds will be of special benefit.

SMALL UNIT LEADERSHIP. This is the responsibility of the team leader and should be included as a part of training as dictated by the principles of leadership. Specifically that of developing a sense of responsibility in your subordinates.

COMMUNICATIONS. The importance of small unit communications cannot be stressed enough. The team must be able to communicate with each other during movement to an objective (and inside buildings) and during the implementation of a tactical plan. One guiding principle in communications is this:

All team members must have individual radios at all times! Any team that goes into an operation without them is facing down an adversary with an empty gun. Therefore, training in radio procedures is invaluable, especially brevity in radio use. Each team should have its own private line and its own code for security reasons.

While radios are essential, the primary method of communications should be nonverbal during movement and clearing buildings. Once contact is made with an adversary silence is no longer an operational necessity.

In considering communications training the leader should ask himself several questions:

1. How do you communicate and maintain silence during movement?
2. How do you communicate during darkness not using radios?
3. How do you communicate inside a house or building while trying to clear rooms, wearing a gas mask?
4. How do you communicate at great distances during night or day without using the radio?

The FBI has developed a set of hand and arm signals that are adequate for movement during day or adequate visibility situations. A team may develop its own signals depending on its ingenuity. However, if the team adopts the FBI signals, supporting units will more than likely understand them.

Binoculars are useful to see at great distances. Every leader should carry them.

A difficult problem occurs when it is dark or a time of limited visibility. If a team member shouts, the security of the team will be jeopardized. Several methods are suggested.

1. Red lens flashlight. A red lens flashlight can be used with an appropriate code. It can be seen at long distances in the dark while it does not afford the adversary a possible means of detecting the team. If used correctly, it will work. A red lens penlight can be used if the team is close together. This light is hard to detect unless you know where to look for it.
2. If the team has a night seeing device (the author considers

this piece of equipment a must), either a starlight scope or infrared, hand and arm signals can be used at night.

3. If members are close enough to each other, the touch method can be used. This is especially useful inside buildings. And, of course, a code must be worked out. Inside houses the adversary has the advantage; he knows where he is and may more than likely have a good idea where you are. But don't give him any more advantage that he already has. A penlight may also work, but in a limited sense. Never use radios inside a house—too much noise. You can talk if you whisper (this can be done through a gas mask) but the less talk the better, for if the adversary is listening and knows your next move it could be fatal for you.
4. *The Poncho Meeting.* During movement over terrain, a blanket or poncho can be put over two or three men, and by using a flashlight and whispering, communications can be obtained.

The point should be abundantly clear that communications security is essential and training on how to communicate in all of the aforementioned situations is of utmost importance.

Finally, if you want to coordinate an entry without a radio, you may want to carry along a red star cluster flare to coordinate the entry.

How frequently should a team train? This question is often asked. Tactical training should be conducted a minimum of one session a week. This would include communication and hands on equipment training as a part of the tactical exercise. Psychology classes should be taught at least once a month along with firearms training. Leadership training should be an ongoing thing primarily during tactical training. Also, PT is a weekly must!

Of course, the time that a SWAT team is able to train is dependent on each individual department's situation. Leaders should keep in mind that no matter what situation is present, he should train his men every chance he gets.

All training should be performance oriented. This means that in each training session the team should be expected to perform certain tasks, under certain conditions. The training should not be considered adequate if those tasks are not adequately performed. Performance oriented training gives the leader a method of evaluating the training sessions in terms of performing an objective.

PART II
TACTICS

SWAT teams do not move like other police units.

Chapter 4

THE PRINCIPLES OF MOVEMENT

THE PRINCIPLES OF MOVEMENT must never be violated. Once a team becomes lax and moves from its staging area to a crisis area or movement is conducted inside a structure in a slovenly insecure manner, violating the principles of movement, it invites death.

Before beginning the principles of movement to contact or under fire, several terms, later to be employed, must be explained.

ASSEMBLY AREA–STAGING AREA (AA). Both terms describe the place where the vehicle is parked, the team members get dressed, and where the operations order is usually issued. Sometimes this may be where the line authority sets up its command post. (The command post for the team is always the location of the leader.)

RALLYING POINT (RP). A permanent geographical area that is used by the team to rendezvous in case it is split up.

CONTROL POINT (CP). Geographical area that is used by the team leader to control and gauge his movements.

COMMAND POST (CCP). The line authority headquarters usually at the AA.

CRISIS POINT (CPP). The exact location of the adversary.

CRISIS AREA (CA). The area immediately surrounding a crisis site where danger exists because of adversary fire or SWAT tactical operations.

ADVERSARY. The hostage taker, murderer, sniper, felon—Klingon.

CELL. A variation of a SWAT team. Can be a part of a large SWAT team.

PRELIMINARY ORDER (PO). A warning order that alerts the team and puts them into action.

OPERATIONS ORDER (OPORD). The detailed attack plan that the leader gives to the team.

POINT OF DEPARTURE (PD). The last "safe" and "secure" geographical location where the team is located before beginning its movement to contact. Usually at the PD the team stops, reorganizes, and makes any last minute checks before advancing.

ROUTE OF ADVANCE (RA). The route the team will take to the crisis area.

DANGER AREAS (DA). Geographical locations along the route that poses dangers to the team.

ADVANCE TO CONTACT (AC). Movement from the crisis area to a new position (maybe the crisis point) that will likely cause adversary contact.

FRONTAL ASSAULT (FA). Suicide.

AUTOMATIC RIFLE (AR). Cover and entry weapon.

LONG GUN. High powered rifle with a scope.

RALLYING POINT (RPP). A geographical site where a reconnoiter team breaks up, gathers intelligence, and returns to disseminate it.

Now let's begin the lesson of learning to walk before running.

Cover and concealment

The first principles that the team members should always observe are cover and concealment. The object of every movement is to do so without the adversary being able to see the team moving. Ideally, the adversary should not have notice of the teams' presence until after he has been subdued and apprehended by the SWAT team. The uncertainty of a team's presence is as much a factor in their favor as a show of force. If the adversary is firing at a team or if he is watchful and will fire upon seeing you, the principle of cover is important. Cover enables a team to be shielded from an adversary's fire. Cover may be an automobile, a barbecue pit, or the side of a building, even a tree. Cover, besides meaning a physical obstacle between the adversary's fire and the team, also means a team member covering another team member by watching over his movement and firing at any potential adversary that may pose a danger to the advancing member.

CONCEALMENT is important for movement security. During movement the entire route of advance should be designed with concealment in mind. Things that typically are used as concealment are: wooded areas, darkness, automobiles, smoke, and alleys. Concealment should be approached from two ways—day and night.

DAY CONCEALMENT. Besides the obvious use of every obstacle a team can use to conceal them from the adversary's eyes during day movement, two other things must be considered—noise and camouflage. The team should pick a route that will afford them noise security. Wooded areas are especially noisy so movement should be slow and careful. Each step should be carefully considered. Branches and other debris must be held for each team member by the man immediately in front of him. This will prevent him from being slapped in the face or causing noise. Wind and rain, plus loud industrial noises, are good noise cover.

BUILT-UP AREAS (city streets-subdivisions). These areas are less noisy for movement, but do not afford the concealment that trees and bushes (wooded areas) do. Movement through built-up areas should be quick, secure, and quiet. Dogs are a team's natural enemy, both day and night. A good way to quiet dogs is with CS, food, or a good rap on the head.

CAMOUFLAGE. Consider camouflage from the aspect of what will make a team less conspicuous during movement or at stops. Face camouflage can be used, even trees or branches and bushes.

The uniform is always a factor. Nothing should be worn that will reflect light or make noise. Green is best for vegetated areas, and medium gray is best for urban areas.

NIGHT CONCEALMENT. Never move through wooded areas at night if you can help it. The noise of your traveling through wooded areas will overcome the concealment that the woods afford you. Move along the wood line in the shadows. Even on a dark night, with no moon, there will be shadows.

A team can take advantage of the night sounds, such as wind, rain, and even man-made noises while moving in the open terrain on a dark night (no moon). The crisis area can be reached quickly by watching every step and picking up one's feet.

In built-up areas, take advantage of shadows and stay away from street lights and avenues of approach that autos frequently travel. A car light can illuminate a team quite well. Again, beware of dogs and clotheslines. Use sides of houses and move quickly and quietly from one house to another. If the team is caught by a light, freeze and don't move. Most people will not notice you if your clothing is dark and your face is darkened. Again, you should consider light discipline. Never use any kind of light that will give your position away. Sometimes a team will want to use spotlights or extra duty flashlights to illuminate a subject, but in situations such as this the team is not concerned about being discovered.

MOVEMENT ALONG A ROUTE OF ADVANCE. Many forms of advance can be taken. The prime rules to consider are the all around security, cover and concealment, and proper formation.

PROPER FORMATION. All around security and cover and concealment will be insured by proper formation. What formations will be used will be dictated by the mission, the time of day, weather and terrain, and distance from the assembly area to the crisis areas. During the OPORD every team member should be advised of his position in the formation to be used. Sometimes a team will develop an SOP that once a certain type of terrain is encountered the team will automatically assume a certain type of formation.

THE FILE. The file is nothing more than a straight line. The file affords more control to the leader than any other formation because of the closeness of the team. The file should be used in tight alleys, when moving only on one side of the street, or in open or closed (wooded) terrain at night. An elongated file may be used in thick vegetation during the day.

The Principles of Movement

When a team stops every member of the team has an assigned area of security.

THE COLUMN. In a column the team is spread out. The advantage of the column is that more area can be covered. The column is used when the team, though traveling as one unit, is broken down into cells, or when the cells have separate assignments on the same mission. The column is used best during the day, in open areas, or down a city street during the day. The column should never be used at night, in thick vegetation, or when visibility is very limited.

The leader can easily conduct fire and movement or cover and movement from the column (a discussion of this is found in Chapter 5). The leader can extend the team with a column (keep in mind communications).

MOVEMENT THROUGH A CITY. A special problem exists when moving down a city street—team security. Team security is the most pressing single problem that the team will encounter. Danger areas are more frequently on a street than in a wooded or residential area. Alleys, cars, basement apartments, tall buildings, and intersections all pose a danger to the team's security.

DANGER POINTS (DP). DPs are any areas that may subject the team to ambush or discovery. Sometimes discovery is inevitable, but security must never be compromised at a danger point. No matter what a danger point consists of—an opening in terrain where the team is about to emerge from a wooded area, a street intersection, a bridge or an alley—the actions of a team will be essentially the same.

1. The point man must notify the rest of the team of the danger point. (A column is used in this example.)

The Principles of Movement

2. The point man motions for BUM to cover him and the leader moves up to the PMs position. He and the leader discuss the team's next move.

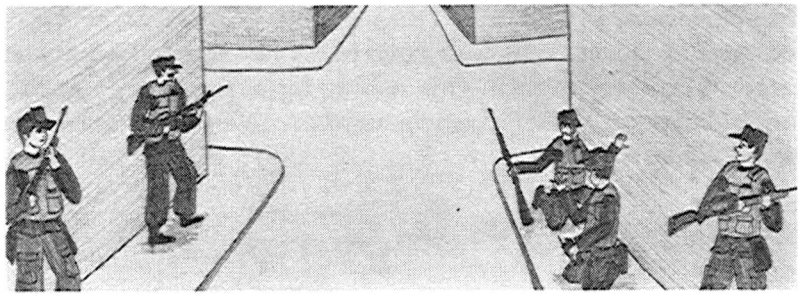

3. Next the BUM and the PM move across the street. The RS will move up to the BUMs position prior to their movement.

4. After the BUM and the PM have secured their positions, the rest of the team will advance at the same time. *Note:* as the BUM and the PM moved, they were covered. They also looked at the terrain they were advancing to, looking for adversaries. Once in position, both covered the movement of the rest of the team, both up and down.

If the team had wanted to turn either corner instead of going forward, some of the members would have to switch positions.

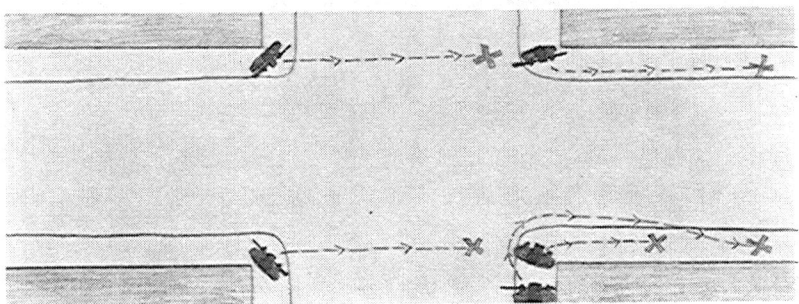

In the above schematic one can see how the team's positions can vary. *Caution:* the leader never changes.

AN ALLEY. This would be handled in much the same way. First, you can simply all cross at the same time (if the alley is small). This will allow the team to move quickly and not give an adversary a shot at you. Once his attention is directed your way, everyone will be across safely. For larger alleys, the first man on the side of the alley brings the next man up and then is covered as he crosses the alley, then covers for the next man and so on. If the alley intersects both sides of the column, this procedure should be done by both sides of the column and at the same time.

Clearing a bridge requires that the point man and BUM clear the super structure (if possible) while the rest of the team gives adequate coverage. If at all possible, bridges should be avoided as routes of advance.

CLEARING AN OPEN SPACE. In a wooded area this is different. When the point man comes to the open space he should stop the team, bring up the leader and the back-up man. The PM and the BUM must then move alternately down the wooded side of the open space, cross over, then check the other side. Once they meet at the trail they then signal the rest of the team which should cross at the same time.

The leader should realize that the key to any action at a danger area is the point man's ability to perceive a possible danger.

Hand and arm signals, penlights, or barely audible whispers should be used to discuss the plan of action. Also, during stops in dense terrain, once the plan of action is devised, or just at a stop to get one's bearing, messages can be relayed front to back by voice.

It is also suggested that teams develop an SOP for the last man in line to send up to the front a count. For example, if you have ten men the last man in line is always number 1. He says one to the next man in front of him, and the next man gives his number until number 9 says so to the leader. This action may be necessary because men have been known to become lost at stops and a team moves ahead without them.

ALL AROUND COVERAGE. Using the column for all around coverage is the basic principle of moving down a city street. Each man is assigned a zone of security responsibility, which he does not deviate from unless his position in the formation changes.

Areas of security responsibility

POINT MAN: His area is always to the front during movement and stops, both upwards and downwards. He also covers any other team members' movement.

BACKUP MAN: Right of a street—up and down. Covers the point man when he moves to a spot for the team to move to.

The Principles of Movement 55

LEADER: All around responsibility
OMNI-MAN: Left side of the street up and down. Covers the leader and prepares to assume point if needed.
REAR SECURITY: Rear security—up and down.

Team members must become accustomed to looking up and down. Snipers can hide in windows high up, and in basement apartments, even under cars and trucks. All around security means just that. The team should move like a porcupine, every angle covered.

WEATHER CONDITIONS. Weather condition will play an important part in what formation the team chooses. For instance, if the day is rainy or windy, movement can be conducted both at night and day through wooded areas or anywhere else with less regard for noise discipline. If it is dark the team can move through open spaces. Snow will illuminate the team so concealed routes should always be chosen.

VERY OPEN TERRAIN. If a SWAT team is ever given the mission to move in open terrain (desert), during the day the wide open column is best (remember in every situation—don't bunch up!), or if at night the modified file is used.

MAP AND COMPASS TRAINING. It should be apparent now that a team should have adequate training on how to read a map and a lensatic compass. This will be more apparent if a team is called upon to move for long distances.

Never move unless another team member is watching your route for adversaries.

Chapter 5

MOVEMENT UNDER FIRE

THE PRINCIPLES OF COVER AND MOVEMENT. The hard and fast rule that must never be violated is that no team member moves anywhere unless he is covered by another team member!

This principle can be employed by individual team members or can be done as a cell or team effort. When performed as a team, communication between the covering element and the movement element must be worked out. The various forms of communication already discussed must be considered. Another factor that is indicative of cover and movement is that with cover and movement, adversary contact is expected, but not yet encountered. The cover element looks for possible danger points that the movement element could be ambushed from. Ideally, these points should be selected before the "OK" is given to the movement element to advance.

In the above illustration the movement element waits until the cover element leader gives them the go-ahead. The movement element never moves until the cover element gives word. *Caution:* Communications security must be considered. An SOP should be developed by the team so that whenever there is to be a movement to contact, or an action at a danger point, the men that need to move will automatically look to the cover element to select targets, then, after being signaled, will move. An SOP of this type is important because the team leadership should be able to react to developing situations almost on instinct. Special problems can be faced during limited visibility or at night. It should always be assumed that a potential adversary can see the team at night. And since cover and movement will most likely be used, even at night, detection is not desired in implementing the maneuver. Therefore, it is essential that the cover element has the capability of seeing at night. This can best be accomplished by the use of night seeing devices. With a device the cover leader can spot adversaries and direct any covering fire needed. If the movement is by individuals (one covering one) the team members must learn the elements of night vision.

Night vision
1. Never look directly at what you want to see, but rather look to the right or the left of it. The sensory nerves in your eyes that enable night vision are called rods and are located on the sides of the inner eye, not in the middle.
2. A substance called "visual purple" is emitted in the eye aiding night vision. If you quickly blink your eyes or rotate them every so often, it will create more visual purple.
3. Always shield your eyes from light at night as light destroys visual purple. Car lights are especially hindering to night vision.

Not only will the cover element be required to cover the group that is moving it must also be able to spot adversaries. It is suggested that a powerful flashlight be employed by the cover element to focus on an adversary, once he is discovered. This sudden light focused on an adversary will startle him and create a diversion that will allow the movement element to get into position.

Discussion of cover and movement inside buildings will be discussed in Chapter 7.

FIRE AND MOVEMENT. The principles of fire and movement are almost the same as cover and movement. The communications between the two elements is somewhat easier since the element of discovery is no longer a consideration. However, control is more difficult since the noise from the shooting of the cover element can cut down on the ability of the movement element to understand their leader's commands. Again, an SOP will help minimize control problems.

Another consideration is fire discipline. The cover element must learn to not fire sporadically, but rather at specific intervals and at a specific target. Remember, the object of fire and movement is to get the movement element to a position without being hit by an adversary. Once the movement element is at the desired location, all firing must stop. How well this is accomplished will depend upon the team's communication procedures. The movement element must inform the cover element of its position. Visual sightings can aid here, but again consider the situation in which darkness and limited visibility affect this. The flashes from the shots of the cover element can destroy night vision. It is suggested that goggles, with darkened lenses, be kept on hand for the covering team. Goggles will greatly reduce the effect of night firing blasts.

Another factor to consider is that in fire and maneuver, adversary contact is expected and may be ongoing. The team must consider the adversary as capable of returning fire. To move under fire is at least difficult. But, if the cover team and the movement team can mass fire at a specific point, the adversary will, in most cases, be suppressed. It should be mentioned that the movement team should only enjoin the adversary with fire as a last resort. Their primary mission is to get from one place to another. Also, they will not be able to spot a target on the run as easily as the cover team. Fire and movement, like cover and movement, can be a one firing for one.

Finally, one prime consideration that teams should remember in choosing weapons is always to select the best weapon for the particular job that must be accomplished.

At a very short distance a shotgun is effective, but for distances of ten yards or greater it is absolutely essential that the covering force use automatic weapons. The AR is best since it lays down enough accurate, rapid fire to cover the men that are moving. Police officers have a natural affection for the shotgun but the love affair with the "alley clearer" must give way to sound tactical consideration that cover and movement and fire and movement demands. Sometimes, it is necessary to fire over the moving officer's head or very close to him in order to save his life. Never be caught covering an officer at distances with a shotgun or you might bring him down too. In addition, during a situation where a hostage may be taken and it may become necessary for a team member to take action at that moment, a shotgun is of no use since the hostage is bound to be hit along with the adversary.

Ricochet consideration always plays an important part in determining the use of weapons. However, a SWAT team leader must learn to think mission-wise. The potential threat that a dangerous, armed adversary poses to the public is greater than possible richochet from an AR bullet. If the area is properly cleared this risk is minimized. Also, for reasons previously mentioned, with the absence of adequate, accurate firepower a fellow team member may die. This maxim should be considered.

> Any situation the team is called upon to resolve will be dangerous and life threatening to both the public and the team. Get the crisis resolved with whatever it takes. In the long run the public will be safer and the team considered more competent.

The team leader and the line leader must work together in clearing areas—but to insure team integrity and safety, the SWAT team should always take charge!

Chapter 6

SPECIAL MOVEMENT SITUATIONS

SPECIAL SITUATIONS. Certain special movements by the team are demanded in some situations, while the principles of cover and movement and fire and movement are always present and the basic formations are always used. Each of the special situations talked about in this chapter require a special addendum to the principles already apostolated in this book.

CLEARING AN AREA. The prime purpose of clearing an area is to keep civilians from becoming involved in the conflict that might occur near the crisis area.

It should be noted that the responsibility for clearing all areas in or near the crisis area is up to the line commander (Patrol, Traffic, or CID). But the SWAT team leader must ensure that this is accomplished for the safety of the team. Therefore, it will usually become necessary for the team to assist, even supervise this operation. The maxim in clearing areas is, "The clearing of an area should always be conducted as if the team is under fire."

The crisis point is always the center of the area to be cleared. The crisis area is the geographical section of land within immediate range of the crisis point, or so near the crisis point as to afford cover and concealment from any adversaries located at the crisis point. In nearly all instances some line units will be present when the team arrives. *Twelve steps in clearing a crisis area are suggested:*

1. Find out the exact location of the crisis point, the adversary, the supporting units, and individual line officers.
2. Find out the exact location of any dwellings or other structures that may contain civilians. (Whether they

are inhabited or not has no significance at this point.)
3. Find out if the crisis point is encircled. If not, take immediate steps to do so, using either line units or the team.
4. Request and get all avenues of approach into the crisis area blocked off to all traffic and all on-lookers. (This may require arrest of citizens or disciplinary action against rubberneck officers on the part of the Chief of Police.)
5. See that adequate fire and medical services are in the area and know their exact location.
6. Develop in as much detail as possible a map or drawing of the crisis area and the crisis point.
7. Develop four approach points leading into the crisis area and request at least five line officers to be immediately marshalled at each approach point. The officers must be told that from the very moment they arrive on the scene they are to take orders from no one except the SWAT team. The importance of this is obvious, once the situation is turned over to the team it must be a controlled mission, no one else must be allowed to interfere.
8. This is the most difficult step. If the adversary is surrounded by line officers, these officers must be immediately put under the control of the SWAT team, and the first orders must be to stay put and not return fire. If the surrounding force is half and half (half SWAT and half line) the SWAT team members must be replaced by line officers under the same orders.
9. The SWAT team should report to the leader and be given detailed instructions and shown a map of the area. Once this has been accomplished, four of the SWAT team members should be sent to each of the four locations where five line officers are positioned. If the crisis area is large and a helicopter is available, it should be employed. The SWAT team leader, if at all possible, should conduct the clearing operation from a helicopter where he can easily observe all the action.

10. The line authority should position itself at the command post (the area where the SWAT team leader and the line superior first meet) and keep in constant communication with the SWAT leader. During the clearing operation, the line authority should never issue an order affecting the operation without first checking with the SWAT team leader. The mission of the line authority is to coordinate the efforts of the line officers and the SWAT team, and assist in summoning other support services.
11. The line authority superior must remove all unnecessary persons to the outside of the crisis area perimeter. Outside the perimeter, the line authority controls and performs in directing crowds and traffic, briefing news media, etc.
12. The SWAT team leader gives the order to each of the four contingents to start evacuating citizens found in the crisis area, using the principles of movement.

Persons who refuse to leave should be forcibly made to leave since they are potential hostages and the state's interest is greater than that of private property (see *Warden v. Hayden* 387 U.S. 294). Also, every state has an inherent right to protect its citizens and to look out for their welfare. It should be kept in mind that the crisis point may shift if the adversary escapes from his original position and takes up another. However, should this happen, the overall plan should not be affected. The encircling element will simply have to be directed towards another location. Keep in mind that comunications between elements is very important for coordination. The type of terrain of which the crisis site is composed will not cause the twelve steps to be altered. In other words, it is not the terrain or type of crisis, e.g. hostages or snipers, that is important, it is the plan and the leader's ability to put the steps into motion that determines the worth of the plan.

In clearing civilians, officers should pass them hand to hand like a bucket brigade; then visually check the insides of all houses and mark them on their maps as cleared.

Once the area is cleared, the tactical solution can be implemented. The same procedures would be followed if the team is called upon to clear a city street or a high rise office building. With a building you would still select locations and start from there.

RECONNOITERING. The main objective of a recon movement is to gather information about the adversary or the crisis point. The principles of reconnaissance are stealth and deception. A team does not want to be seen or heard.

The factors of weather, time or day, terrain, and the adversary will determine the area of movement, methods of movement, and the formation used.

Noise and light discipline are essential. Men with colds or coughs should be left behind. Nothing illuminating should be on the uniform (which should be as lightweight as possible), and nothing should clang or rattle. (Have each man jump up and down before moving in.)

All of the aforementioned control factors and communications security should be employed and the principles of movement should be adhered to. The real difference between a recon movement and other movements is the actions at the crisis point or area.

ACTIONS AT THE AREA TO BE RECONNOITERED. First, before the team even moves, a geographical feature should be designed as the area rallying point. The point should have both cover and concealment available to the team. Each man should be briefed as to where the point is and what he should do at the point. Recon movements are sometimes interrupted by discovery or ambush. If each man knows where the point is he can make his own way there and meet the team.

Secondly, when the team arrives at the ARP, it should stop and reorganize itself for the eventual mission. From the ARP each man should move out in a different direction (but each man should know the directions that the rest will take for safety reasons). Each man gathers his own estimate of what he thinks is important, as far as hard intelligence is concerned, about the objective (the geographical layout of the area and information and descriptions of any persons involved). Once he is finished he should return to the ARP.

After all of the men have returned to the ARP, each man should then tell the others what he saw. This will insure that everyone knows all of the information gathered. It is important that all the information gathered gets back to the command post in case the team splits up.

The team should not relax on its return journey for the hazards back are as real as those found during the approach. Also, the team should take a different route back.

ENVELOPING AN AREA. Enveloping or encircling an area is essential in order to contain the adversary. A prime consideration in any envelopment operation is that everyone is in communication with the leader so that if a situation develops on the other side of the area, from his location, he can control it.

There are several different types of envelopment:

1. wooded areas
2. buildings and city streets
3. housing areas

All envelopment operations begin with an OPORD at the staging area and then a movement. Movement can be by any means; automobile, foot, or helicopter. The prime rule of consideration when moving from an AA to a crisis area is that no matter what means are used, cover and concealment should be employed.

The team should always approach the crisis point from different directions. This prevents the team from being bunched-up and possibly pinned down by a sniper. Therefore, once the team leaves the staging area together, they must split up at the departure point so that the team will converge on the crisis area

Special Movement Situations

from all sides. Again, the leader must keep in communication with each element of his team in order to know their exact locations.

The team positions itself based on several factors; (1) where it can get adequate coverage on the target, (2) the best position where it can place itself near the crisis point in case a quick entry is needed, (3) visual sighting of each other, and (4) ease of control.

Many times, once the team is in position, adjustments may have to be made in order to satisfy any of the aforementioned tactical considerations. If the team approaches from at least three different sides, ease of adjustment will be realized.

The leader should always position himself where he can best control the situation.

WOODED AREAS. In wooded areas the targeting of the crisis point is very difficult. Snipers or other adversaries can easily conceal themselves. In most cases it will not be the job of the team to locate the adversary. However, if this is the case the following should be considered:

1. Noise moving through a wooded area should be kept at a minimum. Movement from the AA to the different points of entry can best be made by a low flying helicopter or an automobile. Consider the line-of-sight the adversary might possess. Once the woodline is entered, even if the exact position of the adversary is known, movement should be the same as if the team were on a reconnaissance mission.
2. At some point close to the crisis point the different elements should stop and communicate their positions to the leader. This can be done with earplugs for radios. Words can be whispered into the receiver and heard plainly if the volume is turned up. At this point it should be evident that a good course in map reading, compass operation, and land navigation is needed and should be taught to all team members.
3. Sometimes, the advance and control of the elements may be conducted from a helicopter. But if the adversary is a sniper, caution should be used.

4. As the team gets closer to the site, movement should be slower until the point is in sight. Then adjustments in the perimeter can be made. If it is nighttime, a night-seeing device is a necessity.
5. Once the team is in place the crisis point may be marked with smoke. This will give the team members a clear picture of the exact location of the crisis point.

If the exact location of the adversary is not known, the adversary should be located by careful reconnaissance. It should also be evident by now that movement to contact in a wooded area is slow, careful, and quiet.

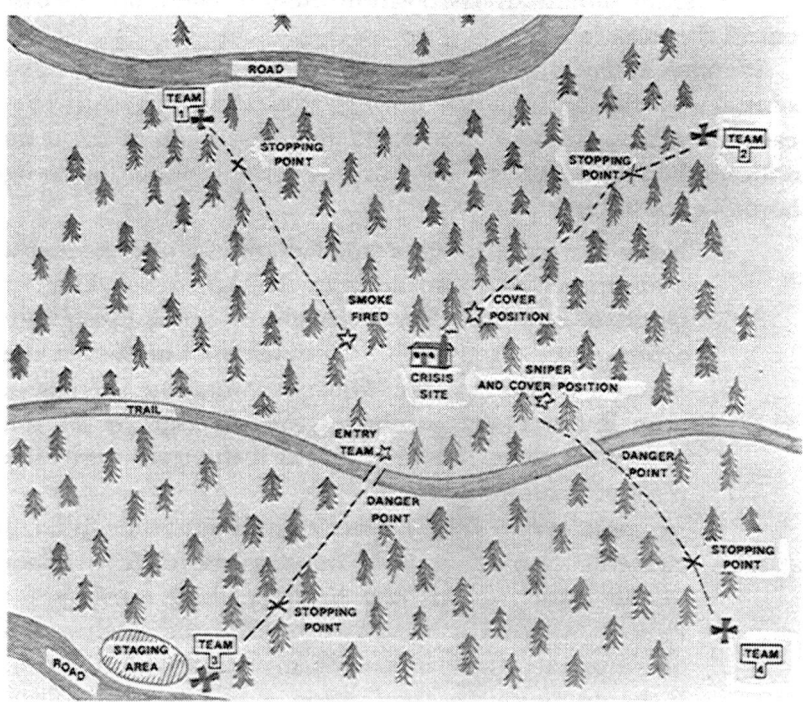

CITY AREAS. The same principles of enveloping a crisis point in a wooded area are to be employed in city areas. Only the terrain is different. If the team uses the principle of movement in cities, the safety of the movement will be ensured. The real difference in wooded and city areas, as far as this maneuver is concerned, is that the team must get the high ground overlooking the crisis point. If the crisis point is a building, the highest in the city, a helicopter might have to be used to cover the movement team as it approaches the building to be encircled. (Building entry and clearing a building will be discussed in the next chapter.) A large hazard in enveloping an area in a city is the large number of civilians that may be present. Line units must assist the team in clearing the citizens out of the area.

A HOUSE. There are three prime rules that must be considered when enveloping a house, and they differ from the other principles of envelopment:

1: All exits and windows must be covered.
2. All gas and smoke projectors must be within range.
3. The team must be positioned in order to make a safe and quick entry if necessary.

A detailed discussion of house tactics can be found in the following chapter.

COUNTERAMBUSH. Once the team leaves the assembly area en route to the crisis area it is likely to be ambushed. If proper movement is observed, including all around security, this is less likely to occur. However, should the situation occur the team should prepare itself to go into an SOP of *immediate ambush reaction*. The first instinct of the team will be to run or take cover. This course of action will be inappropriate.

Many times the ambusher will hit a team at one point hoping to drive them into a certain area where the rest of the adversaries lie in wait. Also, the concealment that is ostensibly available may be in fact lined with explosives or worse.

The area that the team is caught in is called a "kill zone." The area that the team may be channeled into may also be a kill zone. The only place in an ambush site that is not a kill zone is the exact location of the ambusher. The team should, on being ambushed, immediately react by returning a heavy amount of fire in the adversaries direction and by assaulting him with tenacity. Never move away; never seek concealment; return fire and assault; these are the principals of counterambush.

In training for counterambush make the situations unexpected and insure that the team reacts instinctively and spontaneously.

Once the team is positioned around a house the gas mask must be worn at all times, until the mission is completed. All training should be commensurate with this rule to include firearms training.

Chapter 7

CLEARING HOUSES AND BUILDINGS

CLEARING A HOUSE. Clearing a house of an adversary is the most dangerous task of a SWAT team. Adversaries usually know the layout of the house, they conceal weapons in favorite hiding places, and they hide in the places known only to them. Most important, they have the advantage of surprise over the team once it enters the house. When entering a dwelling the team must ensure that it is not ambushed by a hidden adversary. To insure that this will not happen and that the adversary may be eliminated no matter where he is in the house, this chapter will go into detail with many ways to turn the natural advantage the adversary may have around in favor of the SWAT team.

Before moving to any crisis area wherein the crisis point is a house, certain actions at the assembly area are imperative.

First, find out who is in the house and as much information as possible about the adversary or adversaries. Also, what type of crisis is this: barricaded subject, heavy arrest, hostage situation, etc? What type of weapons does the adversary have? Are there any innocent persons in the house? If so, who are they? What are their ages? Do they have any known medical problems, such as heart ailments or respiratory ailments? Also, what type of house is it? Try to find out from relatives or neighbors the layout of the inside of the house. Gather as much information available about the immediate area surrounding the house.

Once this information has been gathered, and disseminated to the rest of the team, a temporary plan can be formulated. Employ the team leading procedures, the most important of which is the leader's personal reconnaissance of the crisis area.

After the leader's recon, the team should be moving into position with constant communications established with the leader. Remember, adjustments will normally have to be made. As the team moves into the area, it should be simultaneously cleared of innocent persons (see Chapter 6). Also, the principles of envelopment should be followed. It will be easier to envelop a house during the night rather than during the day because of concealment. It might be necessary during the day to lay down a smoke screen (smoke grenades) to conceal the team's movement.

At this point the team should be in position with the leader mentally selecting an entry point and making a temporary plan.

It is proper now to leave the team at this juncture and briefly discuss the aspects of different situations that can occur when the crisis point is a house.

HOSTAGES OR INNOCENT PERSONS IN THE HOUSE. The SWAT team should never be involved in the negotiation process unless several members are designated as negotiators only. The team's primary job is to conclude the crisis tactically if negotiations reach an impasse. (The particulars of freeing hostages will be dealt with in Chapter 10.) One thing that must be considered is that the team must develop a plan that will insure the safety of the hostage(s). Gas can be particularly harmful to elderly persons, children, and persons with respiratory or circulatory ailments. This should be considered before firing gas into the structure. Also, never use shotguns where there are innocent persons located inside the house. If you shoot the adversary, then the hostage or innocent party may be hit also.

HEAVY ARREST—FELONIES. When a subject is to be arrested, two situations can arise: (1) sometimes the subject is not aware of the police presence. If this is the case, deception and stealth should be employed in enveloping the house, and the tactical plan should have as its main emphasis surprise and shock. (2) The subject is aware of police presence. The prime rule to consider is this—if he is alone (without innocent persons), never go in and get him even if you can. Time is on your side. Use gas. However, sometimes this will not work, and the team may be forced to go in and get him. The details of this will follow. Diversion and a quick and safe entry should be employed. It should be mentioned that the team must never be involved in the arresting process. This is the responsibility of the line officer. Once the mission is completed, the team should be free to go back on call and should not be tied up in booking.

BARRICADED SUBJECTS. In most instances this is the criminal who has been caught in the commission of a crime or a mentally deranged individual who may be shooting at citizens or police. The same principles in a heavy arrest where a subject is aware of police presence should be used. The team should never fire back at a subject unless given the green light to do so and then only if a clear shot is presented.

SNIPERS INSIDE A HOUSE. This is the most dangerous situation that may face a team and the citizenry. In most instances the sniper will be well armed, intent on taking a life, and has little regard for his own life. He must be eliminated quickly. The tactical plan has to be carried out with force and tenacity. The prime rule in sniper situations is to suppress his fire with the team's fire. (Sniper and hostage situations will be dealt with in Chapters 9 and 10.)

Now let us return to our team which has now enveloped the structure mentioned earlier. We are going to assume that an entry has to be made and that no innocent persons are involved (although the tactics would not vary if innocent persons were to be involved, just fire high).

MOVEMENT FROM THE ENVELOPMENT POSITION TO THE POINT OF ENTRY. In order to safely clear any house, either at night or during the day, there are some devices that the team absolutely must have: (1) periscope, which enable a team to look into rooms before entering; these can easily be made and should be adjustable; (2) a flashlight, to attach to the periscope at night and to illuminate rooms; and (3) a light source; the best is cyalume, a chemical light that burns for thirty minutes at 40 watts. The team never enters a darkened room without lighting the room up with something. Cyalume will do this and will create a diversion before entering (see later discussion). Also, some doors will swing open and then automatically shut by a hydraulic hinge. Take a small two by four or find something in the house to keep this door open. And upon entering, one officer may have to force and keep the door open with his body.

A point of entry must be decided on. It will usually be a door, but can be a large window or other entrance. The entry team should be only two men, with the leader following them. The rest of the team should remain in position to catch any adversary that may flee outside the house.

Before the team enters, gas (if used) should be pumped into the house. A smoke screen (if during day) should be put in front and back, and a loud diversion (grenade simulator) should be set off opposite the entry point. When the entry team moves it should be covered by the rest of the team.

Clearing Houses and Buildings

Smoke, if used, should be thrown fifteen seconds prior to the entry and the grenade simulator just prior to entry. Goggles, with tinted lenses, should be worn if the grenade simulator blast is near enough to destroy night vision.

Never move in front of windows and doors. Sometimes this may require team members to crawl to the entry point with the team firing over their heads.

If gas is fired, the team should consider that a fire is possible, and an escape exit should be designated if officers are already inside the house. Also, gas can cut off oxygen. If enough is fired into a room, a subject will pass out and then he can be carried out on a litter. Team members should consider this also. In addition, never use smoke inside a structure. It blocks your view as well as the adversary's view.

GAS MASKS. These should be put on once the team is in position. If the team is wearing baseball-type hats they should be turned around and worn over the mask.

THE ENTRY. At this point the entry team should, only for a moment, get its bearing and then enter quickly. If the door is locked, it should be kicked in.

Clearing Houses and Buildings 81

A small battering ram, or a pipe with handles, can be used. This is to be used with safety in mind. Carrying a small battering ram can be difficult, but it can be used to prop a swinging door open once you are inside the structure. This can be especially useful if you need to use a periscope and you do not want an officer to hold the door open for you.

The FBI suggests Porta-power speed saws that pry open doors and hydrajets that use pressured water. However, these devices would be more useful in buildings or apartment houses where doors are usually stronger than an average door. In some instances a small blasting charge might be needed to blow open a locked door. If a door swings toward you sometimes a simple nail with a piano wire attached to it can be driven through the door opening with the butt of a gun and the door can be pulled open.

Once the door is open, entry should be done very quickly with a maneuver called the criss-cross-over.

As each man enters he must quickly cover his area as indicated. If he finds the subject confronting him, the necessary action should be taken. The team leader should initially stay at the entrance. Before any entry is made, a diversion such a cyalume, a beer can, or white handkerchief should precede the officers. If this is done, the suspect, if he is present will have his attention diverted for just a second and that is all the team will need.

Now the team is inside. If it is dark, the suspect will not be readily visible (gas masks can reduce visibility) and there will, more than likely, be a mist from gas (if gas is used). Remember, the suspect knows where he is, you do not. If you do talk, it must be in whispers. Gas masks will not interfere with you talking in a whisper. However, you must consider that you should not give away your intentions, and the best way to do this is to let a hiding suspect hear you. If it is dark, hand and arm signals will be unavailable to you so the team must develop a good communications procedure for inside houses at night. A small red lens pen light, if used properly, will provide some communication (beware the adversary may see the light too). The touch method, a working signal between two men is also suggested. The point is—communication is going to be difficult, at best, inside a house at night. And, if you don't know where the adversary is located, you must find him and not give away your location. Be quiet, move quietly, never illuminate yourself against windows or open doorways. If possible, turn on lights as you make your way through the house. But, if you do turn on lights make sure that you use good cover and movement procedures. Stay close to the walls, use furniture, if you can, but don't trip over furniture. Keep in mind that even if you can turn on lights there will be parts of the house where you will not be able to turn lights on because of safety reasons. No matter, before you enter any room toss in cyalume or a flashlight then check the room out with your periscope. *Periscopes and artificial lights are a must—don't clear houses without them.*

Again, some rooms will not be designed for the use of a periscope and will have to be cleared without its aid. However, never enter a darkened room without using artificial light. And, if you have a subject covered in a room, and he is alone and of no danger to anyone but himself, don't charge in, pump gas in, exhaust his oxygen supply, then bring a stretcher in and carry him out. You must first locate the subject.

The schematic below is the most difficult house anyone could be asked to clear. The entry team is at its initial position. It is dark and the adversary could come at them from almost any direction.

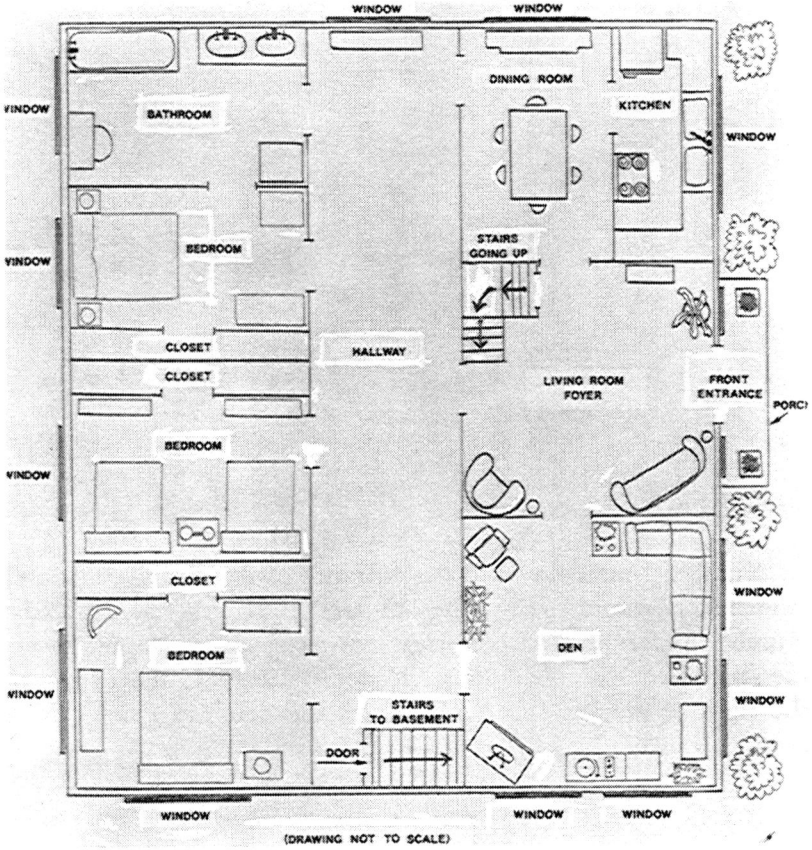

The officers chose to go to the right. They could have gone left, but they didn't. The point is, go only in one systematic direction to clear a house. Remember, each room and closet must be cleared.

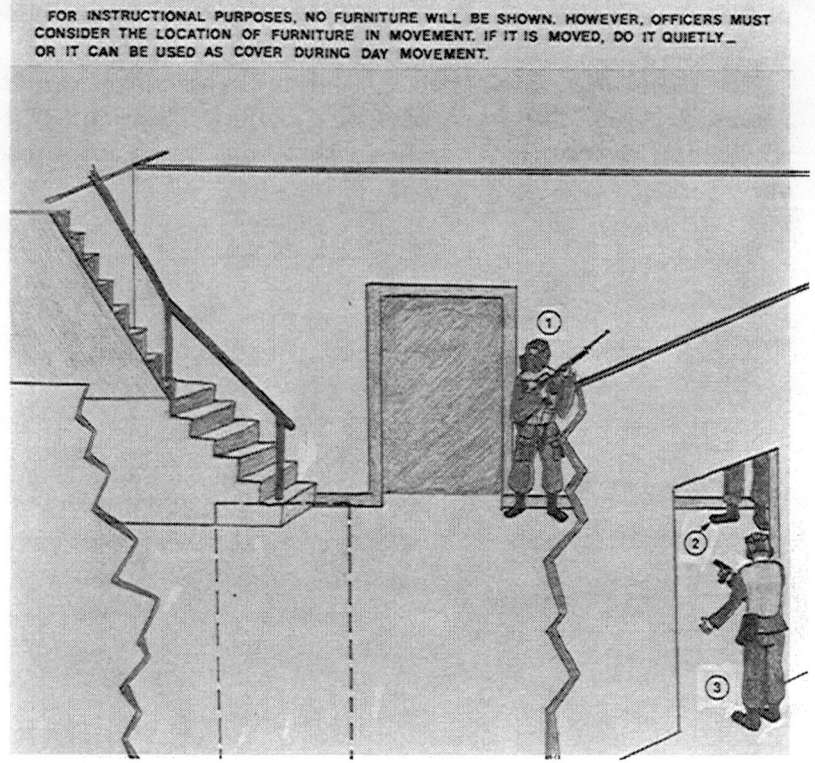

FOR INSTRUCTIONAL PURPOSES, NO FURNITURE WILL BE SHOWN. HOWEVER, OFFICERS MUST CONSIDER THE LOCATION OF FURNITURE IN MOVEMENT. IF IT IS MOVED, DO IT QUIETLY— OR IT CAN BE USED AS COVER DURING DAY MOVEMENT.

Number 1 man moves to the entrance of the dining room and crouches, he should cover the stairwell, but only momentarily. Number 2 man moves to the right corner of the room and covers the stairwell. Number 3 man (leader) enters and moves just to the right of the entrance. He covers the den, hall, and dining room entrance.

Clearing Houses and Buildings

Next, number 1 man and number 2 man check the room out with the periscope, after throwing in cyalume to illuminate it. They then execute a room entry movement. The first man always goes low, the second high. SOP should determine who is first.

Number 3 man will then move to their former position and cover the stairwell, hallway, and den entrances. Once inside the room, number 1 man covers the entrance to the dining room and number 2 man covers the kitchen entrance. At this point, number 3 man radios for the outside man (number 4) to come into the house and take up a position at the door so that any movement in the den, hallway, dining room, or stairwell can be detected after the team has left those areas. He will be number 1, 2, and 3 man's rear security.

It is important that before any team enters, it must create a diversion. A quick toss of a light, a handkerchief, or even a beer can will create the diversion and maybe give the team the edge on a nervous adversary.

For just a second the adversary, if he is in the room, will look at the light or the other object. That is all the team needs. He may also fire at the object instead of the team. A grenade simulator will also work and give a shock effect before entry.

Back to our problem.

Clearing Houses and Buildings 87

Next, 1, 2, and 3 should line up next to the outside of the kitchen wall, with number 3 covering the hall entrance. Number 1 and 2 then execute a side by side entry after first using the diversion.

Next, number 1 and 2 move to the hallway entrance with number 3 covering. After 1 and 2 have moved, 3 will get behind 2.

Number 1 and 2 will execute an entry with 1 covering the hallway and bedroom areas, and 2 taking the right side of the hall, then the entrance to the bathroom. As 1 and 2 cross, 3 should cover the bathroom door then drop back.

At this point 1 and 2 will cross over the hall and enter the bathroom. Number 3 man will move just into the hall and cover the hallway and its exits.

Then each room should be systematically cleared by 1 and 2 until they reach the last room across from the stairwell leading to the basement. At that time the leader (3) should come down the hall to the entrance of the foyer and signal 4 that all is clear. With 3 standing at the entrance, 1 and 2 should cross over and clear the den.

Whenever the team has to cross over an open space such as a hallway or open door, the one profile silhouette method should be used. This allows for quick, covered movement to the other side.

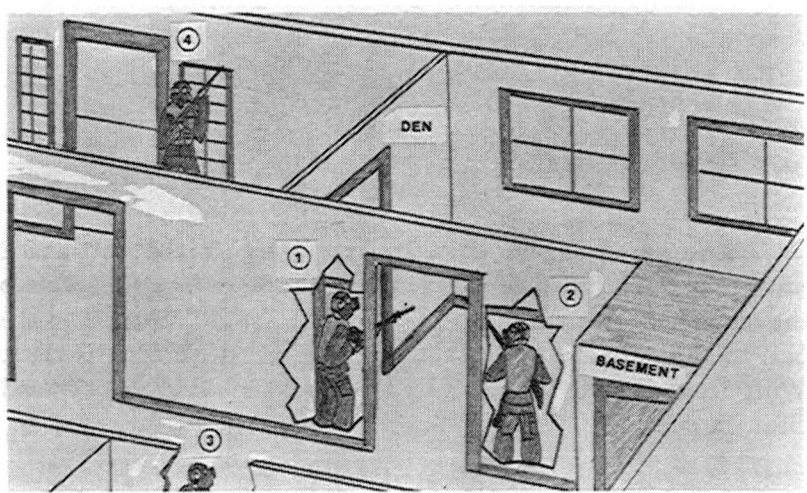

Next 1 and 2 should move to the hallway entrance to the den while 3 moves down to the left side of the hall and covers the basement entrance.

Next, 1 should move across to the hall behind 3. Number 2 man should move along the wall with his weapon trained at the bedroom door.

At this point all three members must move at the same time. Number 3 and number 1 man should execute a room entry into the bedroom while 2 wheels around and covers the stairwell.

At this point it should be obvious that the adversary is not on the ground level of the house. Furniture should be checked as well, and closets are cleared in the same manner as rooms. Number 2 should be left to secure the stairwell leading to the basement, while 1 and 3 join 4 and prepare to climb the stairs.

Climbing stairs presents a special problem. Once the team is able to safely get up the stairs, the rooms on the second floor will be cleared in the same manner as the first.

Clearing Houses and Buildings 93

But, first the team must safely climb the stairs! Stairwells are hazardous because the adversary has the advantage of looking down at you. The following are the FBIs suggested ways of climbing stairs.

When an open stairwell is present, one man lies on his back covering the open part with a pistol. He slowly inches his way backwards until he reaches the top. Another team member moves below him, covering his back. As the man on his back moves upward he taps the ankle of his cover man when he is ready to move.

When the door at the top is closed, one man crawls toward the top with a cover man at the bottom. Another man may follow with an opening device, if the door is locked. If the adversary should suddenly open the door, he can be taken under fire by the cover man. Always use the sides of stairs to place your weight on, never the middle where squeaks can occur and always go up on the *door handle side*.

BASEMENTS. Under no circumstances should a SWAT team enter a basement. Unfortunately, one's head is located at the top of the body, and in order to cover a basement entry properly, the anatomy of our bodies would have to be changed. However, the basement may be viewed by throwing in an artificial light and using the all-important periscope. If it is clear, then of course entry can be made, but even this can be dangerous.

The best way to clear a basement is to flood it. Use foam from the fire department or send in a K-9 (police dog). Normally, never use dogs to clear a house; they are not discriminatory about who they attack.

ATTICS. Most attics have very narrow entrances. If stairs of normal width are available, use the techniques already discussed. Again, before entering use a light source and use a periscope!

Teams should realize that entering and clearing houses is necessary in most instances. Departments cannot simply burn down every house an adversary is in. If the house is approached and entered safely, and each room is systematically cleared, using cover and movement, the dangers that are present will be lessened. Clearing a house is slow and dangerous.

BUILDINGS. Buildings pose a special problem since they cannot be destroyed. They will have to be cleared by the SWAT team. The prime rule in surrounding buildings is to take the high ground.

Clearing Houses and Buildings 95

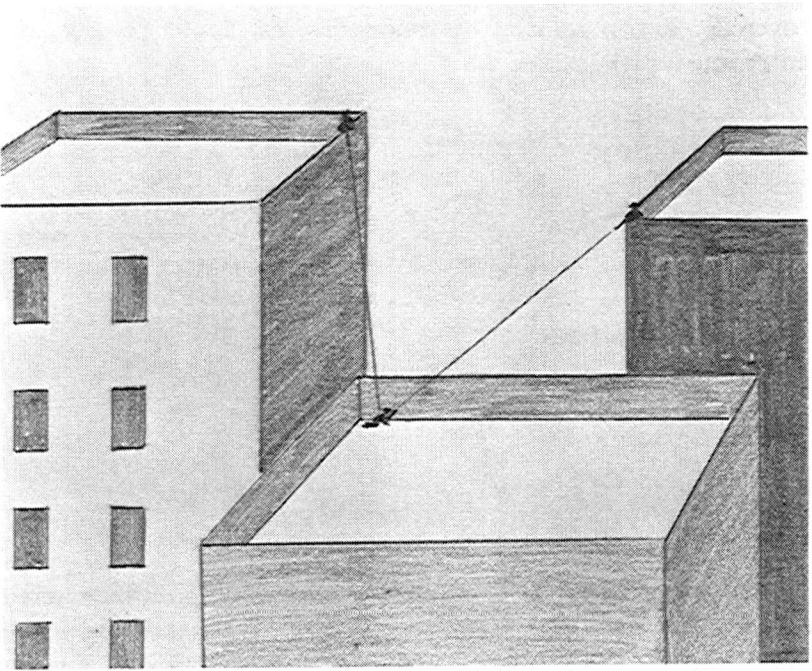

Other buildings surrounding the crisis point (target building) may be entered by elevator or helicopter, whichever is safer. The exits at the bottom of the building should be covered by SWAT team members, if possible. But more than likely patrol units will do this because the area is large around a building. The crisis area should be cleared of all civilian personnel and this includes any buildings within the range of the adversary.

Buildings are never entered from below if this can be avoided. The adversary should be driven down into the street. Sometimes, if a sniper is on the roof, this will not be possible. This presents a special problem that will be discussed in Chapter 9. We are only concerned at this point with the entry of the building.

The absolute best way to enter a building is to land on top by helicopter and have the team exit there. Even if the adversary is firing out of a window or holding up in a room on, let's say, the third floor, the landing can still be made on his blind side. Nearly all buildings will have a roof entrance. If this is open it should be used with caution. The adversary may have it locked or covered. Periscopes and diversion devices should precede any entry into a roof entrance.

If the roof entrance is locked, the building should be entered on the floor where the crisis area is located, but always on the blind side of the adversary. This can be accomplished by using fire escapes, if these are located on the blind side. However, this method can never be relied upon. Therefore, the main method of entry might have to be to rappel down the side of the building and enter a window on the blind side. Army TC 90-6-1 deals with rappelling which is easy and fun, but safety should always be observed.

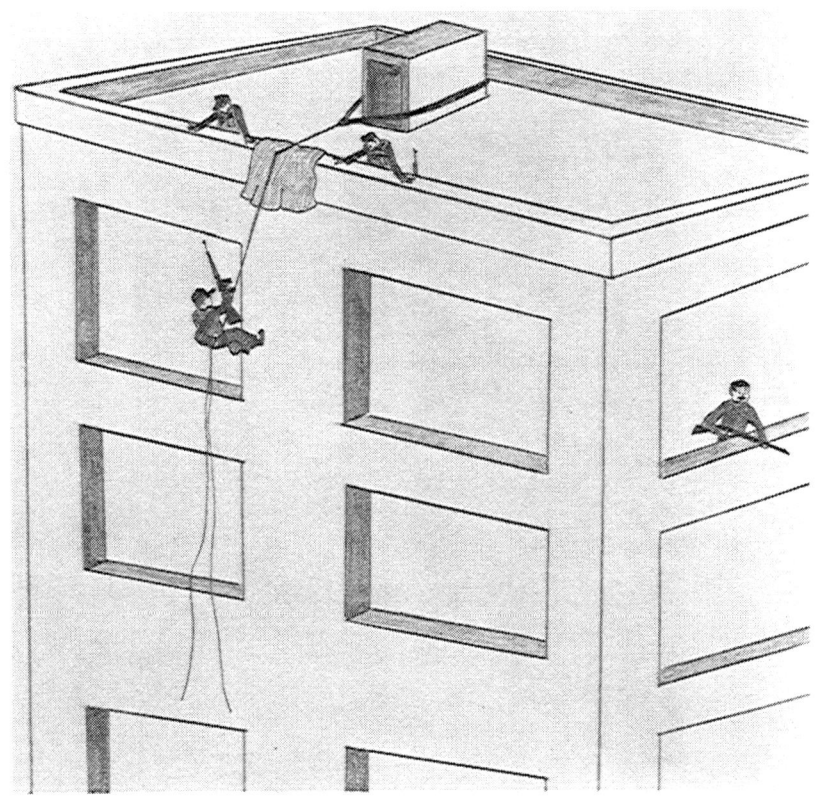

Sometimes a building may not be tall enough to rapel from, and no roof entrance may be available. Team members should then try to enter the upper floors by hand methods or grappling hooks. Grappling hooks afford a good method of entry if they are accurately made and the entry is covered by the men on the ground.

There are many methods of lifting a team member up to a higher level to effect an entry.

Clearing Houses and Buildings 99

1. Weapon Method

2. The Hand Method

3. A team can also use an aluminum ladder that can be extended.

Many times buildings must be crossed in order to envelope the crisis point. When a member crosses over a wall separating buildings, he should roll over it, never step or climb over it. A roll-over lends to less exposure against the skyline.

Also there will be situations in which officers must climb down walls or out of windows. The FBI has developed what they call the "spider crawl." It is a very good method to effect a drop. When you fall you nearly always land straight up.

Once an entry is affected into the building, each room and hall should be cleared as in a house clearing situation. Elevators should almost never be used as electricity may be cut off. Also, the adversary might be waiting for your arrival as the door opens.

If stairwells must be used then the precautions mentioned before should be considered, but stairwells because they are obviously accessways (obvious to the adversary) should be approached like the second story of any house. The same principles of movement should be used. Sometimes it will be necessary to enter on the floor where the adversary is located since continued use of stairwells can be hazardous. Periscopes should always be used to go down stairwells. Usually stairwells will have levels. They may be cleared as shown in the illustration.

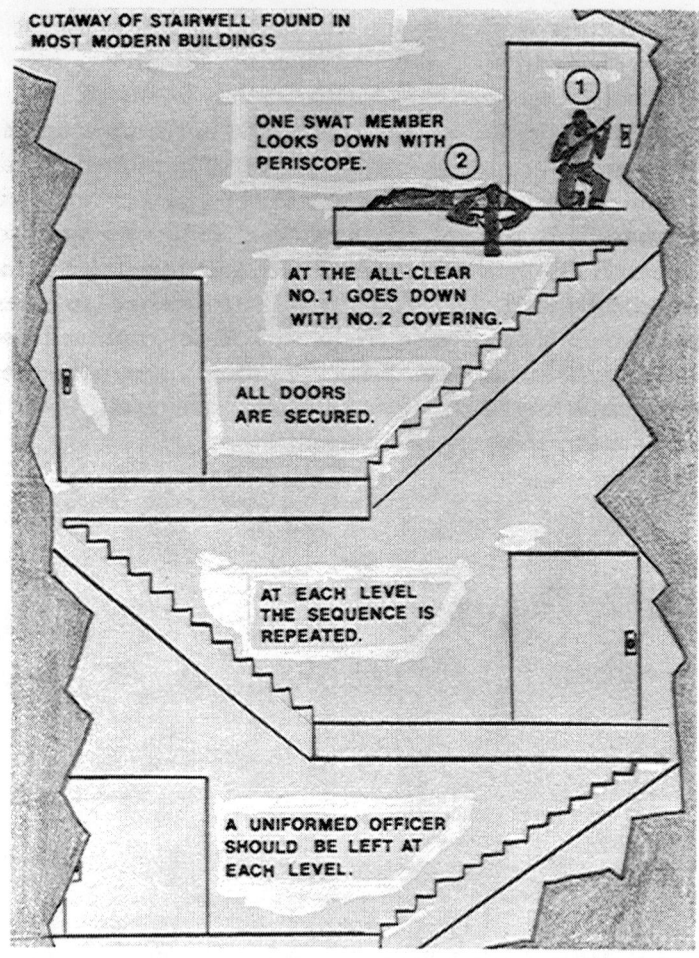

At this point the SWAT team member should drop the periscope. If it is all clear, another member should go down quickly with his gun ready to encounter any adversaries. At every level this process should be repeated.

When the team affects an initial entry at the top of a building, the exits in which all stairwells empty into should be entered at the bottom by line units with communications to the SWAT team leader. Thus, while the team is clearing a particular level, the adversary will not effect an escape. The SWAT leader should make sure that all areas at the level they are clearing are indeed clear, and additional officers should be brought in from line units to guard all cleared stairwells and exits. In other words, the team's rear must always be covered.

FIRING WEAPONS INTO WALLS. In both houses and buildings there may be times when the adversary's exact whereabouts is known to the team, and it is also known to the team that in order to get him out a fire fight is going to be necessary. Most double ought bucks in shotguns and AR ammunition can penetrate standard sheetrock walls. An officer's life may be saved by shooting through a wall. But, beware, the exact location of the adversary should be known, and there should be no innocent parties with him.

Actions at the assembly area should be organized and systematic.

Chapter 8

ACTIONS AT THE ASSEMBLY AREA

ONCE THE team arrives at the assembly area, they should find the vehicle located in a secure place. Newspaper men and on-lookers must be kept at a distance (this is the responsibility of the line commander). The team should have one member designated as the supply officer. It is his responsibility to issue equipment according to SOP or special equipment at the direction of the leader. This will preclude any possible confusion.

The assistant team leader (or the next ranking man) should start checking each man's equipment and temporarily organizing the team for action. He should then make a communication check within the team and with other units.

Weapons should be checked and cleared. Ammunition should be adequately issued (never run out of ammo). Pyrotechnics and gas should be issued to members who will need it.

When the SWAT team leader returns from his initial meeting with the line commanders he should make sure that the following is done:

1. The area around the AA is cleared of all unnecessary police and civilian personnel.
2. Fire, medical, and public utilities are on location.
3. A helicopter is standing by.
4. Traffic diverted to other routes.
5. A line officer is guarding the SWAT vehicle.
6. Ascertain if there are any injured persons in the area that have been taken care of.
7. Ascertain if any contact with the adversary has been made.

It should never be the responsibility of the SWAT team leader to do any of the above. The leader should then give his OPORD and prepare to move out. If possible, pictures of the adversary should be shown to the team before moving out; if not, an adequate description of the adversary should be given to the team members. CID detectives should assist in finding out about the adversary's background. Also, if possible, a departmental psychologist should be called to assist in determining the mental makeup of the adversary.

The key to good assembly area action is the adequate preparation of the team itself. Never have to go back to the SWAT vehicle unless absolutely necessary; try to take everything you will need with you.

Also, before leaving the AA, each member of the team should be briefed on what is happening and what he is expected to do. Then when you are ready, notify the line units that you have left the AA and are heading for the point of departure.

Actions at the Assembly Area

This would not have lasted long with a SWAT Team on call.

Chapter 9

THE SNIPERS

THE SNIPER represents the most absolute danger that can face any SWAT team. It should be understood right from the very beginning that the mission of a team in a sniper situation is to kill the sniper quickly before he kills someone else. A sniper has one goal in mind—to kill. There is no room for discussion about his intentions. He is out to kill, and in nearly all situations he doesn't mind dying. The tactics of the team should be aimed at seeing that he doesn't take a team member or an innocent person with him.

Snipers can strike from anywhere, but in most cases they will take to the high ground, whether it be the top of a building, a hill crest, or a tower.

SWAT teams should always try to get above the sniper, while the line units are clearing the area within the range of the crisis point.

Movement from the assembly area to the crisis area must be made with extreme caution as the team will be an exceptional target for the sniper.

The team should be split into at least three contingents. Each must be assigned a high area in which the sniper can be observed. At least three long guns with scopes should be carried along with an AR-15 (no shotguns!). This will give the team maximum range and impact should an assault be needed.

It is important to keep in mind that the high ground might not be accessible, so any structure that will put you closer to the sniper is good. (Caution, make sure that whatever you use, i.e. building tops, hills, or towers, etc., gives you cover and concealment.) Once in position, the sniper should be targeted by all three contingents with communications to the leader.

The Snipers

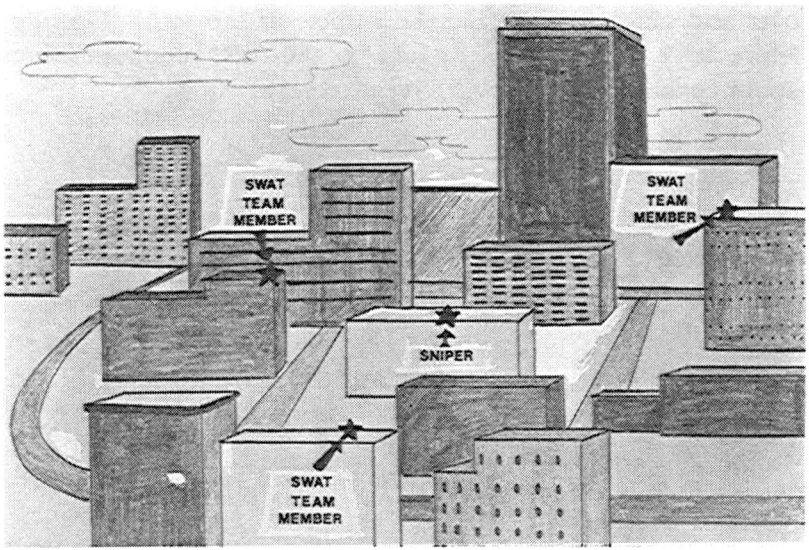

Once each man on the team possessing a long rifle has the sniper in view the leader should give the order to fire at will. Remember, the purpose of the team is to eliminate the sniper. A clear shot should always be taken advantage of.

It does not matter where the sniper is located. If he is in a wooded area, use the technique mentioned in enveloping areas. If he is in a house, use fire and movement (keep him pinned down). If he is on a building top, keep his head pinned down with fire, and if he presents a good target take it off. However, you might be required to enter a building to eliminate him. There are three methods of entering buildings to take out snipers.

ROOF ENTRANCE. In this situation, the elevator from the top, although undesirable, might be tried, but be prepared to fire when the elevator door opens. A roof entrance might be used, but there is always a possibility it might be locked. The team must take the necessary tools to effect an entry of a locked door. Once you open the door a diversion may be needed such as a grenade simulator. If you have an ordinary fragmentation grenade it may be thrown in to precede your entry (only if the sniper is alone). After the explosion, make a quick crisscross and employ cover and movement to take the sniper off the roof. *Caution:* Before any team member sets foot on the roof, communications should be made to the firing element to cease firing.

ROOF ENTRANCE FROM ROOM BELOW. Entry to the roof can be made by throwing a grappling hook on to the top and climbing out of the window to the roof. Two hooks should be thrown at the same time. This procedure can be done only if the sniper's exact whereabouts is known at times and his whereabouts should always be on the opposite side of the team. Fires should be lifted once the team starts the maneuver. Officers should always have good rope, tying them to a stable object in the room they are using. This is the most dangerous and least suggested method to use.

The Snipers

USE OF A HELICOPTER. The importance of the helicopter in eliminating snipers cannot be emphasized enough. If you take two helicopters and hover them off in different directions from the roof with an expert marksman, in most situations the sniper can be eliminated. The marksmen should use AR-15's with normal sights. High powered rifles with scopes are not suggested since the helicopter will have to adjust for winds and the process of hovering will always be a little rough. But if the shooters keep up rapid fire at the sniper he can be hit. The sniper will be forced to choose one of the two choppers to shoot at. When he turns toward one chopper, the other will get him. Whenever the sniper aims at one chopper then that chopper should take evasive action.

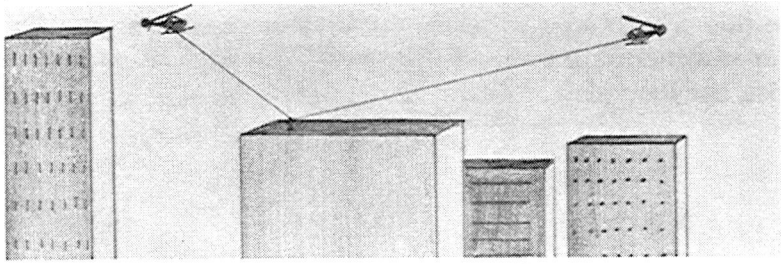

If all else fails, a National Guard helicopter gunship can be summoned and in a very few quick minutes eliminate your sniper problem. Do not call a US Army helicopter. The federal *Posse Comitatus* Law prohibits use of federal authorities to aid local law enforcement efforts.

Remember, the key to eliminating snipers is a step by step method: (1) evacuate the crisis area; (2) encircle the sniper, using the high ground, if possible; (3) with communications ever present, suppress his fire with your own; (4) in limited visibility situations use a starlight scope to locate him and illuminate his position with powerful lights (set away from officers) or blind him with helicopter searchlights, and (5) using deception, surprise, and shock enter his lair.

The Snipers

Special situations require special solutions.

Chapter 10

FREEING HOSTAGES

TAKING HOSTAGES. This is the crime of the future. Hostage takers use innocent people to achieve their own distorted ends without regard to the hostage(s) as persons. Hostage takers see hostages as things, not people. Hostages are merely tools to achieve whatever purpose the hostage taker has designed for his plan to accomplish. There are basically four types of hostage situations that a SWAT team may be called upon to conclude.

CRISIS SITUATION. This is where a person, usually a member of a family, holds the rest of the family or a member hostage to outwardly express to the world some frustration or carry out some neurosis. It can also be a person who has simply been pushed beyond the limits of his endurance by some internal or external pressure. Taking an innocent person hostage is to him the only way that he can show the world he is important and that his problem matters.

PSYCHOTIC OR INSANE PERSON. The psychotic is usually a thrill seeker. He may rant and rave about some political or social purpose for his actions, but his main purpose for taking a hostage is to be important, get a "high," or a thrill, and manipulate society. Being a deviate can be fun. If the person is insane, and suffering from some psychosis, he will be beyond reason and extremely volatile and dangerous. He may have conceived some fantasy idea about why he is taking hostages that makes perfectly good sense to him albeit no one else.

A CRIMINAL CAUGHT IN THE ACT. In this situation, the hostage taker when he started out on his criminal action had no intention of taking any hostages. He might have simply wanted to burglarize a home, or rob a store, or even flee from a traffic ticket. But now he has been discovered and cornered. He sees the hostages as a chance to get out of this trap. He will usually do whatever is necessary to survive. He is the least dangerous of the hostage takers.

THE TERRORIST. This type of hostage taker will be the toughest, most dangerous, and probably the deadliest situation a SWAT team can come up against. Terrorists are for the most part professionals. They purposefully take hostages to express to the world a political aim or cause. The terrorist will fight and he does not mind dying.

The best method of releasing hostages is by negotiation. It is not the purpose of this book to teach the principles of hostage negotiation. The SWAT team itself should never be involved in the negotiation process. The SWAT team should be ready with a tactical solution to the problem if the negotiation process should fail.

The first step in every hostage situation is encirclement (envelopment). Once the crisis point is encircled and the crisis area cleared, the team leader must gain as much information about the hostage taker, the hostage, and the physical layout of the structure or terrain being used by the hostage taker. The leader must have this information before he can develop a plan. He should also be made aware of the progress of negotiations at all times.

Once the team is in position, and after the leader has gained the needed intelligence about the entire situation, he should begin to formulate a plan. The plan to free the hostage must be one that can adapt to change, for hostage situations can change by the minute. The team must be ready to implement a tactical solution to every hostage situation it encounters should negotiation efforts fail.

During negotiations the team should do nothing, not return fire, not move unnecessarily, absolutely nothing. The hostage negotiator is in charge. The team's job is to isolate and contain the subjects. It should be kept in mind that hostages can be held anywhere. In houses, buildings, laundromats, apartments, bus terminals, buses, airplanes, a lone automobile, schools, trains, and even police stations. But basically, the principles of enveloping a structure would apply to nearly all of these places. Trains, cars, and planes pose a special problem which will be dealt with in more detail later.

Some hints in formulating a plan:

1. Hostage takers almost always try to stand over their hostage to obtain a commanding position. Upon entry, fire high, and instruct the hostage to stay down!
2. The hostage will usually be kept in one place. Find out where.
3. In terrorist situations, do not depend upon the killing of the leader as a means of disrupting the organization and morale of the group. They understand the principles of the chain of command.
4. Consider the effects of gas on the hostage.
5. Never use smoke inside a building. This will prevent you from distinguishing between the hostage and the taker.
6. Do not depend upon the hostage helping you.
7. The longer the situation, the better the chance of surprise and shock because the hostage taker will be tired.
8. Your plan should be designed around surprise, shock, quickness of entry, and deception.
9. You should prepare for the fact that the hostage taker is willing to kill the hostage and he will. Your entry may take the life of a hostage, but without your entry more hostages will be killed. Psychologically prepare yourself and your team for this.
10. If the hostage taker and his hostage are leaving the crisis site and the green light is given to shoot the taker, make sure you: (1) know who the hostage taker is; (2) are in the position to shoot; and (3) have the right man with the right weapon.
11. Center your plan on the best way to save the hostage and eliminate the hostage taker.

If the crisis point is in a house or a building, the aforementioned procedures concerning envelopment and entry should be used. Each room should be cleared with the points discussed in this chapter kept in mind.

The critical point in the operation is the entry! The entry must be quick and shocking. Diversions opposite the entry point are of great value. Do not try to use smoke inside, but rather outside the structure. Take into consideration darkness inside the house and what type of light sources are available to you.

Entering each room of a house where hostages are is a sticky problem. Consider the advantages the taker has in knowing where he is. Make sure that you have the all-important periscope and lighting source. If the hostage taker fires at a member while entering a room or the structure, your return fire must always be high. Never enter a room until it is first cleared by a periscope.

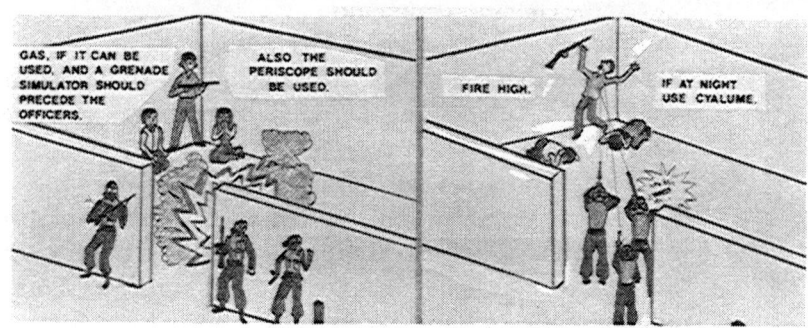

If the hostage taker is using his hostage for a shield, don't go in! This would be suicide for you and homicide for the hostage. Of course, if the hostage taker is killing the hostage(s), you will have to take the bull by the horns for he cannot shoot at them and use them for a shield at the same time. If you are quick enough his fire will have to be diverted towards you and that should eventually be the end of him. If he is just using them as a shield, throw as many gas grenades as you can into the room and cut off the oxygen supply of everyone present. After the gas goes in, be prepared to follow it if you hear shooting. If the gas forces him to come out, he will bring his hostage with him. Prepare, in this case, for one well-aimed shot.

Remember, if the hostage taker starts to kill his hostage(s), the team's quick entry and firing may take the life of the hostage, but will also kill the adversary and perhaps save other hostages from sure death. Stay low, enter quick, and fire high.

Hostages have been taken into automobiles. In this type of situation the key to eliminating a hostage taker, who cannot be made to give up through negotiations, is a well-amied shot from a sniper's round. The back of the head where the medula oblongata is located will best cut off motor nerve responses. It is the back bottom of the head.

The common term for taking persons hostage in a plane, train, or bus is highjacking. The principles for freeing hostages on a plane, once it is on the ground, can equally apply to trains or buses. There is more visibility on a bus, thus a sniper round may be the final solution to consider. So we will now deal with planes.

One of the first things you have to remember about a plane is that it is highly explosive and flammable. Each wing is filled with aviation fuel and the materials it is made from are flammable. Also, once the plane has touched down its doors may or may not be open. If the doors are open they may be the worst way of entering the plane, but they may be the only way through. The principles of fire and movement, as well as quick entry, shock, and diversion should be observed.

The best way to enter the plane through an unopened entrance is by blowing the door *or use the outside latch.* This will make the entrance a surprise since the terrorists will have to cover the open or closed regular entranceways. Once inside, again, fire high. Most of the hostages will be made to sit down in the seats of the aircraft. Usually the hostage taker will be standing at or sometimes near the cockpit, or he could be in the very back of the plane.

Some suggested ways to effect an entry are on the following pages.

First, approach the airplane at night or early dawn, if possible. Use ladders to assist a quick entry. It will take more than a five-man cell; ten men are suggested. A diversion may be used, but it should be quick and closely timed to the entry.

The entry itself must be quick and shocking, filled with noise and light. All team members should wear sun-lens goggles to protect their night vision.

Once inside, a grenade simulator should be exploded (maybe is should precede you, depending on the situation). This will create shock waves, noise, and a blinding light. No gas should be used as this will create panic among passengers that should be kept stable in their seats.

After the explosion and entry, the hostage takers should be easy to identify because they will be firing back or moving around. The passengers will usually be down in their seats. Remember, shout upon entering, "passengers stay down."

Be sure to clear all restrooms. At this point, information should be quickly obtained from the passengers and crew as to whether any hostage takers are in the restrooms or anywhere else. If a hostage taker is in the restroom, shoot through the wall.

Next, you must go to the cockpit. Again, information from the crew will help. The plane will not have enough time to take off. It takes more than the short time that this operation will take to start a plane and take off (or just take off), even taxi very far. The hostage taker in the cockpit will already have his hands full with the pilots and the thought of the SWAT team coming to his rear, trying to kill him. Again, fire high when you enter. The pilots will be seated and should put their heads down as a normal reaction. Gas may be lobed in to cut off oxygen, but this may expose a member to unnecessary fire. Still, consider gasing the cockpit.

Some points to remember when executing this type of operation are:

1. Never use shotguns, only short ARs or pistols.
2. Attack the plane at night or early morning.
3. Rehearse the whole operation, if time permits.
4. If the attack must be made during the day, a diversion might be needed to help you approach the plane. Consider a smoke screen. If you can disguise your team as medical or airport personnel, all the better.
5. Take ladders with you.
6. Know as much as possible about all persons involved with the incident, hostages and hostage takers, and where they are located inside the plane.
7. Blow an entrance, grenade simulators thrown in, and enter quickly (using goggles).
8. Fire high and short burst.
9. Gather quick intelligence from the passengers and crew.
10. Clear restrooms and cockpit.

No one said that rescuing hostages was going to be easy. But it can be successfully done if certain principles are followed. If a team knows how to move, how to enter, and what diversions and cover it has available, it has a good chance of success. Practice and plan for all of the possible problems that could occur. The key to hostage freeing is training . . . and more training.

Finally, keep in mind that the best solution to hostage freeing is negotiation; but if that fails be ready to implement a tactical solution.

SWAT team exists to assist the officers in the street. Each member must understand and accept this principle.

Chapter 11

THE POLITICS OF A SWAT TEAM

POLITICS CONCERNING a SWAT team is both internal and external. This chapter will try to examine both aspects of the fight that any police organization will have when it trys to establish and keep a highly controversial and explosive organization such as a SWAT team.

EXTERNAL CONSIDERATIONS. Before a SWAT team can be organized the political structure of the city has to be behind it. Besides the obvious problem of funding a team there is the not so obvious political backing. Certain groups within a community will see a team as a group of kill-crazy, "the-gun-is-the-solution" types who enjoy "bagging" adversaries. City Hall has got to be able to withstand this kind of pressure.

The first thing a SWAT team leader, in conjunction with the Chief of Police, can do to help City Hall, is to explain to "the powers to be" the real function of the team. Explain the team's tactics, abilities, and policies. (The team's policy should not conflict with the Police Department's on the whole). When City Hall is made to realize the need for such a team, its uses and capabilities, it will be more able to back the Department. For instance, there is nothing so hot as a sensitive crisis that could not be (or was not) adequately handled because the Department did not have a properly trained unit to deal with the crisis.

In this modern age a police department of any size at all must have in addition to its regular arsenal of crime prevention, equipment, and men, hostage negotiators, and special tactical units to deal with hostage takers and terrorists. The city fathers must realize that the days of "old policing" are over. The adversary is well armed and trained. Most of the time it is innocent people of the community who are affected by his actions. The department must not be allowed to fight with one hand tied behind its back.

One powerful alliance the department can enlist in aid of its objectives is the press. If the news media is given adequate information about the team and is allowed to view training and interview some of the members, whenever the team is called into action the media will have an adequate knowledge of what is going on and will portray a factual presentation of its activities to the public. For in the final analysis city hall will need public support for a SWAT team.

INTERNAL CONSIDERATIONS. Probably as big a problem for a SWAT team as outside pressure from the mayor's office, the press, and the public will be other officers within the department. Developing a SWAT team is to many "old heads" a radical departure from the days when the cavalry stormed the house, and it didn't matter who got hurt. Policing was policing. The best way to overcome this is— (1) make sure the team is properly selected as mentioned at the beginning of this book; (2) be competent, don't let the field men down when the "puckerfactor" is up; good training will aid here; (3) educate the rank and file of the department on every aspect of the SWAT team. This can be accomplished by teaching the tactics, composition, and ability of the team during a regularly scheduled in-service training for all officers in the department; (4) the department should develop a clear-cut policy about the team to include call-up procedure, command at the scene, and the instances in which the team is to be used (only certain calls) ; (5) the policy must have the effect of a general order; and (6) time, this element will work for you in time if the others are followed.

One word of caution: the team leader must insure that the attitude of the team members is one of confidence, but not arrogance. The team in the final analysis is there to serve the line officer and the public.

EFFECT ON THE ADVERSARY. The hopeful effect of the city possessing such a team will be deterrence. Adversaries must be made aware of what will happen to them should they come into contact with the SWAT team. Sometimes, just a show of fire will cause an adversary to give up. Of course, our nation is plagued by an unusual degree of psychopaths who may long for the power of forcing down a SWAT team. But this type will press his luck sooner or later, SWAT or no SWAT.

FINAL THOUGHTS TO FELLOW POLICE OFFICERS

Many things have been left unsaid, but maybe that is as it should be. As mentioned at the beginning of this book, each city's SWAT team should develop its own tactics, SOPs, and procedures. I only hope that this book will serve as a cornerstone for those endeavors.

I also realize that, at the very least, some of the ideas and tactical plans, apostolated in this book, may seem radical, even Draconion to the reader, but police work is going to take on a sinister atmosphere in the coming decade and this will require a dramatic change in police thinking. A civil war is going to be fought with the criminal adversary, and he will not be concerned with fair play. We, the people who must fight him, are already bothered by visions of seeing our country foster a lawless society driven by an uncontrollable economy that excludes the poor. We are afraid of a breakdown in the moral code of our people, promulgated by television replacing the family, violence-oriented movies, and nothing to combat it, as once did the church and our public education system, which has since become cowardly and inept. We fear a new uneducated, contemptuous, hedonistic youth who are hateful of authority and are driven by the need to gain more material wealth. So, with gloom, we know that we will have to fight this war and that we are neither understood nor appreciated.

International terrorism, a distant, bored youth, and an ever increasing, fresh pool of thrill-seeking psychopaths are infesting modern society. The hostage taker, senseless murderers, and their like will increase, and we will have to deal with them. It is ironic that we, the underpaid, over-worked, and over-looked few will be asked by the wealthy, powerful, and ambivalent to risk our lives for their lives and their interest.

But, it will be done. A police officer is separated from all of the derangement and misplaced perogatives of our society by his belief in himself, his badge, and the oath he swore to uphold upon entering service. There are not many of us in this nation, but when called upon to do our jobs we will. Maybe this book will help us to do this job better if we are given the proper tools.

SUGGESTED READING LIST

Adams, Thomas F.: *The Training Officer's Handbook*. Springfield: Charles C Thomas, 1964.
Schultz, Donald D., Norton, Loran A.: *Police Operational Intelligence*. 3rd Edition. Springfield: Charles C Thomas, 1973.
Watson, Sam D.: *Dogs in Police Service*. Springfield: Charles C Thomas, 1972.
Hand to Hand Combat. US ARMY, FM 21-150; Washington, D.C.
Sutor, Andrew P.: *Police Operations, Tactical Approaches to Crimes In Progress*. St. Paul: West, 1976.
Toch, Hans: *Legal and Criminal Psychology*. New York: Holt, Rinehart and Winston, 1961.
Russell, Harold E.: *Understanding Human Behavior for Effective Police Work*. Beigel Allan, New York: Basic Books, Inc., 1976.
Stoffell, Joseph: *Explosives and Homemade Bombs*. Springfield: Charles C Thomas, 1972.
Evasion and Escape. US Army, FM 21-77; Washington, D.C.
Ranger Training. US Army, FM 21-50; Washington, D.C.
Guerrilla Warfare and Special Forces Operations. US Army, FM 31-21; Washington, D.C.
Combat Training and The Individual Soldier. US Army, FM 21-75; Washington, D.C.
Combat Intelligence. US Army, FM 30-5; Washington, D.C., 1961.
Explosive and Demolition. US Army, FM 5-25; Washington, D.C., 1961.
Grenades Hand and Rifle. US Army, TM 9-1330-200; Washington, D.C., 1966.
Training Officer's Chemical Weapons Blue Book. Federal Laboratory; Pennsylvania, 1976.
Passive, First Generation, Night Vision Devices. U.S. Department of Justice, Washington, D.C., 1975.
Moyer, Frank A., Scroggie, Robert J.: *Special Forces Combat Firing Techniques*. Newfoundland, NJ: Robert J. Haessner, 1971.
Moyer, Kenneth E.: *The Physiology of Hostility*. Chicago: Markham, 1971.
Taylor, Karl K., Soady, Fred W., Jr.: *Violence an Element of American Life*. Boston: Holbrook Press, 1972.
Gibbons, Don C.; Jules, Joseph F.: *The Study of Deviance*. New Jersey: Prentice-Hall, 1975.

Schonborn, Karl: *Dealing with Violence.* Springfield: Charles C Thomas, 1975.

Map Reading. US Army, FM 21-26; Washington, D.C., 1969.

U. S. Army Sniper Training Manual. US Army, TC 23-14; Washington, D.C., 1969.

Ambush Attacks. Maryland: IACP, 1974.

Swearengen, Thomas F.: *Tear Gas Munition.* Springfield: Charles C Thomas, 1966.

Beall, J.R.: *Helicopter Utilization in Municipal Law Enforcement.* Springfield: Charles C Thomas, 1973.

Ferdico, John N.: *Criminal Procedure.* St. Paul: West, 1975.

Counterguerrilla Operations. US Army, FM 31-16; Washington, D.C., 1967.

Army Mountaineering. US Army, TC 90-6-1; Washington, D.C., 1976.

Combat in Built-up Areas. US Army, FM 31-50; Washington, D.C., 1969.

Whelen, Townsend; *Small Arms Design and Ballistics.* Georgetown, South Carolina: Small Arms Technical, 1946.

Hatcher, Julian: *Hatcher's Notebook.* Stackpole Books, 1966.

Adams, Thomas F.: *Police Patrol Tactics and Techniques.* Englewood Cliffs: Prentice-Hall, 1971.

Military Leadership. US Army, FM 22-100; Washington, D.C., 1973.

IACP Training Key #234. "Hostage Incident Response," IACP, Gaithersburg, MD.

IACP Training Key #235. "Hostage Negotiation," IACP, Gaithersburg, MD.

Maher, George F.: *Hostage: A Police Approach to a Contemporary Crisis.* Springfield: Charles C Thomas, 1977.

INDEX

A
Accessories, 11
Advance to contact, 44
Adversary, 27, 43, 128
Aircraft, 121
Alarm, anti-theft, 7
Alley, movement, 53
AR-15, 110, 113
Arrest, 77
Artificial lights, 82
Assembly area, 43, 105
Assignments, 28
Attics, clearing in houses, 94
Automatic weapons, pistol & rifle, 8, 9, 13, 61, 103, 123

B
Back-up man (BUM), 13, 14, 51, 52, 54
Barricaded subjects, 77
Baseball caps, uniform, 10
Basements, clearing in houses, 94
Battering ram, 81
Bearing, trait of leadership, 20
Behavior training, 34
Binoculars, 11, 35
Buildings, 94
Built-up areas, 46
Bullet-resistant vest, 10
Bullhorn, 11

C
Call-up procedures, 29
Camouflage, 9, 46
Cell, 5-man, 9, 12, 43
Chain of command, 28
City areas, 72
Civilians, 27
Clearing, 50
  alleys, 53
  areas, generally, 65
  attics, 94
  basements, 94
  bridges, 53
  buildings, 95
  houses, 75
  open spaces, 53
Climbing stairs, 92
Column, formation, 49
Combat veterans, 6
Command and signal, 28
Command post, 43
Communications, 12, 60, 69, 71, 102
  binoculars, 35
  formation, 54
  hand and arm, 35
  houses, 82
  poncho meeting, 37
  receiving mission, 29
  security, 58
  snipers, 110
  starlight scope, 37
  training, 35
Compass training, 11, 55
Control, 12
Controlled team, 12
Control point, 43
Coordination, 28
Counterambush, 73
Courage, 20
Cover, 7
Cover and concealment, 44, 47
Cover and movement, 57
Criminal, 117
Crisis area, 43
Crisis point, 43, 65
Crisis situation, 117
Cross train, 26
CS—CN, 11, 46
Cyalume TM, 81, 82, 85, 120, 78

D

Danger areas, 44, 50, 53
Day concealment, 45
Decisiveness, trait of leadership, 21
Dependability, trait of leadership, 21
Diversion devices, 96, 114, 120, 122
Doors, clearing, 93

E

Endurance, 21
Enthusiasm, 21
Entry
   criss cross, 81
   roofs, 111, 112
Enveloping an area, 70
   city, 72
   hostages, 118
   houses, 73, 77, 78
   wooded, 71

F

F.B.I., 26, 28, 35, 93, 100
File, formations, 48
Fire discipline, 60
Fire escapes, 96
Fire and medical, 28, 106
Fire and movement, 60
Firearms training, 34
Firing through walls, 103
Flashlight, 36
Formations, 48
Friends, 27
Front security, 12
Frontal assault, 44

G

Gas (see CS-CN), 11, 14, 73, 76, 77, 78, 119, 120, 122, 123
Gas mask-(M-17), 10, 74, 80, 82
Goggles, 11, 61, 123
Grappling hooks, 11, 97, 113
Grenade simulators (see Diversion devices), 78, 79, 123

H

Hand signals, 82
Hands on training, 33, 34
Hard armor, 11
Heavy arrest, 77

Helicopter, 30, 66, 70, 71, 96, 106, 113, 114
High powered rifle, 7
Hostage situations, 30, 34, 67, 76, 117, 118
Hydra-jet, 81

J

Judgment, trait of leadership, 22
Justice, 22

K

Kill zone, 73
Knife, 10
K-9, 94
Knowledge, trait of leadership, 22

L

Ladder, use of, 123
Leader (CDR), 14, 19-31, 55
Long gun, 44

M

Map training, 55
Mechanical skill, 6
Medulla oblongata, 121
Mentally deranged, hostage takers, 117
Mission, importance of, 28, 29

N

Night seeing devices, 59, 61

O

Omni-man, (OM), 14
Operations order, 27, 31, 44, 45, 48, 70, 106

P

Penlight, 11, 37, 54, 82
Periscopes, 11, 82, 85, 96, 102
Physical training, 33, 39
Physically fit, 6
Point of departure, 44
Point of entry, 78
Point man (PM), 12, 50, 51, 52, 54
Politics, 127, 129
Poncho meeting, 37
Porta power TM, 11
Posse Comitatus, 114

Preliminary order, 29, 44
Proper formation, 48
Psychologically sound, 6

R

Radio, 10, 35
Rallying point, 43, 44
Rappelling, 96
Rear security (RS), 15, 55
Reconnoiter, 30, 68, 69, 72
Restrooms, clearing, 123
Richochet, 62
Rifle, 7
Roof entrance, 111, 112-115
Rope, use of, 11
Route, 20
Route of advance, 44

S

Security, 3, 12, 15, 49, 54, 55, 69
Selection of equipment, 6
Selection of team, 5
Service bags, 11
Short automatic weapon, 8
Shotguns, 61, 64, 77, 110, 123
Sidearm, 9
Small unit leadership, 33, 34
Smoke grenades, 11, 78, 79 ,120
Snipers, 56, 67, 70, 77, 109-115

Spider crawl, 100
Stairwells, 92, 101, 102
Standard operating procedure, 27, 48, 60, 73, 85 ,105
Starlight scope, 11
Structure of team, 12

T

Tact, trait of leader, 24
Team leading procedure, 29, 76
Tentative plan, 29
Terrain analysis, 30, 54, 55, 124
Terrorist, 118 ,119
Train as a team, 24
Training, 33-37
Traits of Leadership, 19-25

U

Uniforms, 10
Unselfishness, trait of leadership, 23

V

Vehicle, selection of, 6, 7

W

Warden v. *Hayden* (States power over private property), 67
Weapons, 7-9, 61
Weather, 27, 55
Wooded area, 71